Osprey Modelling • 9

CW00349609

Modelling the IS Heavy Tank

Nicola Cortese

Consultant editor Robert Oehler
Series editors Marcus Cowper and Nikolai Bogdanovic

First published in Great Britain in 2004 by Osprey Publishing, Elms Court, Chapel Way, Botley, Oxford OX2 9LP, United Kingdom.
Email: info@ospreypublishing.com

ISBN 1 84176 757 3

Editorial by Ilios Publishing, Oxford, UK (www.iliospublishing.com)
Design: Servis Filmsetting Ltd, Manchester, UK
Index by Alison Worthington
Originated by Global Graphics, Prague, Czech Republic
Printed and bound by L-Rex Printing Company Ltd

04 05 06 07 08   10 9 8 7 6 5 4 3 2 1

A CIP catalogue record for this book is available from the British Library.

FOR A CATALOGUE OF ALL BOOKS PUBLISHED BY OSPREY MILITARY AND AVIATION PLEASE CONTACT:

Osprey Direct UK, P.O. Box 140, Wellingborough, Northants, NN8 2FA, UK
E-mail: info@ospreydirect.co.uk

Osprey Direct USA, c/o MBI Publishing, P.O. Box 1, 729 Prospect Ave, Osceola, WI 54020, USA
E-mail: info@ospreydirectusa.com

www.ospreypublishing.com

Photographic credits

Unless otherwise indicated, all of the photographs in this work were taken by the author.

Acknowledgements

I would like to thank the following people:
Andrew Dextras – for the constant encouragement and great support throughout this project. In particular, I wish to thank him for taking the time to help out with final photos of the completed models. Graeme Davidson – for his objectivity and constructive criticism. Nikolai Bogdanovic and the Osprey team – for their patience and understanding of the labour involved in this project. Dan Oldfield – who enthusiastically contributed to this project by supplying the superb colour 'step-by-step' plates for the Dragon ISU-152 build. Gabe McCubbin of Iwata Medea – who provided me with their Iwata Custom Micron airbrush and Smartjet compressor, which were used to paint and detail the models displayed. Loci Anthian of Great Models Web store – who kindly supplied many of the model kits and supplies featured in this book. Ruben Tam of Amour Track Models – who was ever so kind to send me a set of the JS-3M tracks featured in this book. I hope he appreciates the final results. Valeriy Potapov and his fantastic 'The Russian battle-field' website – for providing me with a wealth of photos and diagrams that helped me resolve building challenges pertaining specifically to the IS-2 build. Swedish model master Ulf Andersson – whose masterful 'destroyed' models served as my inspiration for creating the 'abandoned' IS-2. Also, Sammy Dwyer, Mic Bradshaw, James Blackwell and Jon Bailey for their support and encouragement. And finally, I would like to dedicate this book to my wife, Nancy, whose tireless support and encouragement made this book possible.
Nicola Cortese, January 2004

A word on nomenclature

The Iosef Stalin (IS) tank is also known as the Joseph Stalin (JS) tank. In this volume, the form 'IS' is standard, following the correct transliteration, although some references remain to manufacturers that use the 'JS' form – hence the reason why the occasional discrepancy may appear.

Contents

Introduction

'You never get a second chance to make a first impression' is a phrase that came to my mind many times when working on this project – my first foray into the world of writing. For this reason, I can assure you that this volume has received all the love and care I can possibly muster! I've been building scale armour models seriously for just over four years now, and from the outset I have focussed on doing everything to the best of my ability, be it learning about scratch-building or thinking of new ways of maximising the potential of simple tools. I have asked myself if this book will encourage or discourage modellers from tackling the often extensive building aspects of some of the projects here. Ultimately my humble goal, of course, is to encourage the reader to try things that they may not have done before, and hopefully inspire you to try out new techniques – just as I have been, and still am, influenced and inspired by many other modellers. Some of the projects are best suited to intermediate modellers, while others will appeal to those wanting to sharpen their scratch-building and painting skills for large-scale projects. I also hope this book will act as a sort of reality check for modellers who want to start major build conversions without knowing what may be involved, and give some healthy insight into what to look for when building.

Modelling the Iosef Stalin tank

The Iosef Stalin tanks were some of the most widely used tanks ever produced by the Soviet Union. First developed in 1942, this series of heavy tanks went through World War II, the Cold War and the Arab–Israeli wars in the 1970s. Post-war IS-2s, and IS-3s, were exported to China, Cuba and North Korea. Some of the vehicles played a major role in the outcome of World War II, going head to head with some of the larger German heavy tanks such as the Panther, Tiger and King Tiger, and earned the Soviet Union engineering respect for having built these impressive war machines. The subject matter is thus an important one for modellers.

Another point of interest to modellers is the fact that there were many variants that used the same or similar chassis (the IS-1, IS-2, ISU-122, ISU-152 and IS-3, for example) – giving us a variety of schemes, markings and models to work with. There are numerous kits available of almost every model variant, plus a plethora of accessories and replacement upgrades. Due to its strong appeal, Soviet armour still has manufacturers releasing many variants, new and old, keeping up with modellers' demands.

For this volume, I've chosen to feature seven models, namely the early IS-2, the infamous IS-3 and IS-3m, the brutish IS-152 assault gun, and the rare ISU-152 (mod. 1945) self-propelled gun. There is also a 'special section' featuring a pair of small-scale (1/76) versions of the IS-2, one featuring scratch-built fenders and added details, the other being an 'out of the box' build. I hope this will add an interesting angle to the overall content, considering the tiny nature of these kits. Interestingly, each model is quite different to the others, yet they all feature the same type of building and painting techniques. I've chosen to avoid extended historical discussions and precise timeframes, simply because I want to keep things focussed on the modelling. Most of the kits featured are not linked to specific units or battalions. Some will argue that both history and amour modelling should go hand in hand, and that one must be historically precise – I agree wholeheartedly. However, in this particular volume I want to showcase my models and techniques on an artistic level first and foremost.

Ultimately my goal is to concentrate on the specifics, and hopefully plant the odd seed of inspiration along the way. I've also avoided adding figures and the like to the featured kits, again to help concentrate on the featured kits.

Some principles of building and detailing

First and foremost, I've learnt from some of the finest modellers today that a 'system' of building is vital for good end results – indeed, it is the only way I've found that one can achieve acceptable standards. Some differences are obvious between modellers, in terms of preferred techniques and methods. For me, reading Tony Greenland's seminal work *Panzer Modelling Masterclass* really blew me away: I was impressed by how great an 'all-round' modeller he is. I was greatly inspired to go the extra step in terms of detailing: anyone serious about modelling should have this volume on their bookshelves!

Styrene is by far my favourite material for scratch-building. Before attempting any sort of scratch-building, my advice is to 'start small', adding a strap here, or a rod there. I can assure you that once you've tried this material and technique, you won't look back: it's fun, and the only thing stopping you is your imagination. Check out your local hobby shop for Plastruct or Evergreen styrene plastic: these come in all shapes and sizes. I also highly recommend that any budding scratch-builder should check out the 'train' department in their favourite hobby shop – or even better, visit a hobby shop that specializes in train models. You will discover a great source of detailed accessories that train modellers have been using for years, and which are great for applying to armour modelling.

Tools

Equipping yourself with proper tools doesn't necessarily mean going out and buying the newest, hottest tools on the market. In fact, all the tools I've used in this book are items that I acquired over four years ago, when I first got into armour modelling – something that you can see in some of the photos! You'll find that most modellers have much the same tools and accessories in their arsenal as I do: here is a basic list of what I use.

- Iwata Custom Micron airbrush
- Iwata studio series 'Smart Jet' compressor

In my view, the Iwata Custom Micron is one of the best airbrushes on the market today, being easy to use and maintain.

My punch set – every modeller should have one of these, although I also use plastic train bolts and nuts. These tools are vital for scratch-building.

'The Chopper' – another great item, giving a sharp, even cut for all your styrene building projects.

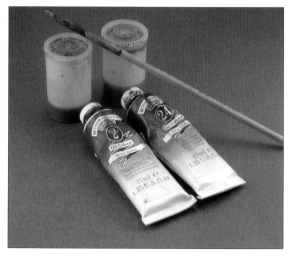

You have a choice of two Mr Surfacer viscosities: the 1000 for a thinner filler texture, and the 500 which is a bit thicker for heavy texturing.

Applying washes to models is an established technique. Just thin with mineral spirits and go!

- Historex punch sets (Bolt and Hex)
- 'The Chopper' cutting board, made by North West Shortline
- Dremel 'Mighty Mite' rechargeable drill
- Numerous Dremel and dental drill bits
- Mr Surfacer 500 and 1000
- Winsor and Newton artist oil paints
- 2 pairs of pliers
- 2 metal rulers
- Sanding items (sticks, paper and files)
- Nail clippers
- Xacto knives
- Tamiya regular and extra thin cement
- Testors liquid cement

Building the ISU-152 in 1/35

Subject:	ISU-152
Model by:	Nicola Cortese
Skill level:	Intermediate
Kit:	DML JSU-152 kit no. 6803
Additional detailing sets used:	CMK Czech Master 152mm ML-20 Howitzer replacement Barrel
Markings:	Eduard Express Masks no. XT 027
Paints:	Tamiya XF-2 Flat White
	Tamiya XF-61 Dark Green
	Tamiya XF-69 Nato Black

In this chapter, we will look at some basic, simple upgrades to Dragon's JSU-152 kit, and focus on a special painting technique for a worn winter wash. Initially, I planned this particular project as a simple 'out of the box' build. However, I felt that this was would be 'cheating', denying the reader an interesting and informative project. I decided to use this chapter as a platform to show how to dramatically enhance detail by using simple, easy to master techniques and sparing use of aftermarket items. Ultimately, it is the modeller who decides how far to go with any given project, and what I'd like to do here is just open the door to several possibilities.

The aim is to enhance and improve the already excellent Dragon kit. Initially released in the 1990s and reissued a number of times since, this kit (as per the complete DML line of Stalin family kits) has proven to be both popular and accurate. This is a perfect kit for anyone who desires an armour kit with flawless fit and ease of building.

Raising the lower hull

One key fault with Dragon's entire IS series of model tanks is the fact that the lower hull sits too low, making the tracks too narrow and too close to the kit's

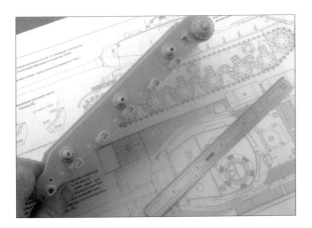

After reading about the height issues with this kit I made sure to check a number of scale drawings. These confirmed that the kit is way too low.

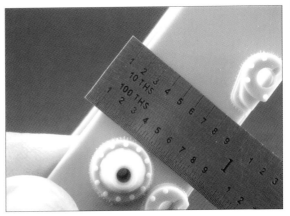

I carefully measured the amount required for adding height, roughly 1.8mm

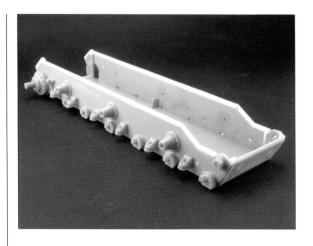

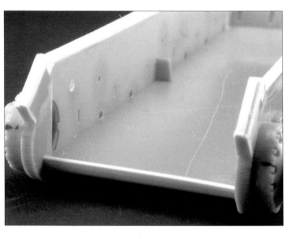

Raising the upper hull makes a world of difference. Note that the rear lower plate of the vehicle also has to be raised to compensate for the height adjustment. Adding a simple styrene strip to the bottom of the lower rear hull plate will achieve this. The front hull will need to be filled and smoothed afterwards.

Also remember to raise the twin step edge in the rear. If you miss this area, you will be aware of a noticeable gap here when attaching the top and bottom halves together.

upper hull. This height issue can be overcome by adding strip styrene to the lower hull and raising it by 1.8mm, as per accurate scale drawings found both in *Ground Power* issue No. 76 and the Russian publication *Armada* issue No. 6 (see the *Further Reading* chapter). I can't understand why Dragon, or any other independent aftermarket producer for that matter, has not addressed this issue. That said, it's an easy adjustment to make, and should only take a few hours.

The upper hull

Soviet vehicles of World War II often had their fenders damaged or even completely missing in a relatively short time. As so often is the case, a simple approach is often the most effective: here, for example, removing the fenders creates a dramatic and realistic effect.

I simply cut the selected areas with my Xenon cutters. After some careful sanding, it looked quite convincing. I decided to go all the way and remove the

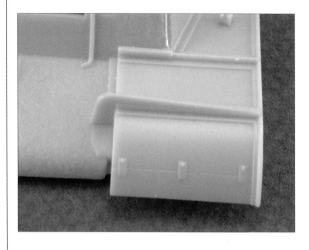

This shows the kit front fender before its removal.

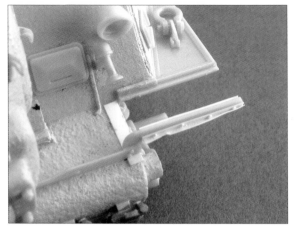

Here is the kit front fender after removal. I kept one of the front fender bracings in place, and sanded and scraped off all the bolt detail. I replaced this with bolt detail using my Historex punch set and added 0.05 styrene sheets to represent the thin metal.

back fenders too: this was also very common with these vehicles and will add a lot to the final look, especially when the massive tracks are in place.

Mud, mud and more mud

Adding dried, caked-on mud to the inside of the hull, the undersides and the wheels is a great way to improve the overall look of the vehicle, especially since the vehicle is set in a winter environment. The tracks will also be weathered up in this way, a great technique shown to me by my good friend Andrew Dextras. The accompanying photos show how to do a simple road wheel. When the upper and lower hulls have been glued together, it is a good idea to add some surface texture to the front plate, to create a smooth, uniform look. Tamiya putty is perfect for this, as it dries nicely and can be sanded afterwards too, to create even more texture. After some light sanding and smoothing out with the Dremel, a couple of coats of Mr Surfacer 500 sealed the front plate perfectly.

The kit road wheel is a good example of how to apply a simple caked mud technique. Brush a little Tamiya thinner onto an area where you would like to replicate the appearance of mud.

Gently drop a bit of powered pastel (I used a dark blue pastel here to provide a nice contrast) onto the still wet area, wait a couple of seconds, and then blow away the excess pastel chalk.

What you have left is your caked mud! Just wait a while before painting, and use a light colour such as Tamiya XF-57 Buff. This can be applied in many areas, like wheel wells, tracks, etc.

Tamiya putty was liberally applied to the front hull with a toothpick. As you can see from the styrene strip, there is quite a difference in height.

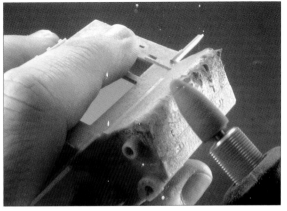

Sanding the front area smooth is easy with a Dremel drill. With a couple of stippled applications of Mr Surfacer 500, the cast texture will return.

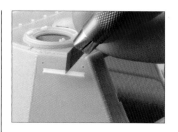

Using a styrene U-brace, measure the distance for the grab handle. This will create a template for duplicates to follow.

Making brass grab handles

There's a simple way to make multiple sets of brass grab handles. Firstly, I drilled out the holes for the grab handles: the position mounts are moulded in place and I didn't want to loose their placement when I started sanding. I usually like to replace the grab handles with 0.19 brass: the step-by-step photos show how it is done.

Adding rear upper plate texture

To add texture, you can apply either Mr Surfacer slow-drying glue, or putty. There is another interesting way to get a 'pock-marked' effect, shown in the photos on page 11. The next time you visit your dentist, ask him or her for any unwanted drill bits that may be destined for the garbage bin – they are extremely useful for all sorts of modelling applications!

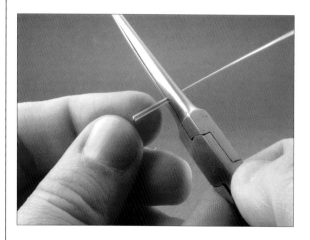

After the first initial bend of the brass grab handle, position your pliers as shown and bend. The styrene U-bracing shape acts as a perfect guide for consistency every time.

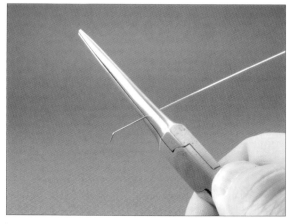

Drop the styrene bracing and, keeping the pliers firmly in place, bend the brass rod into shape.

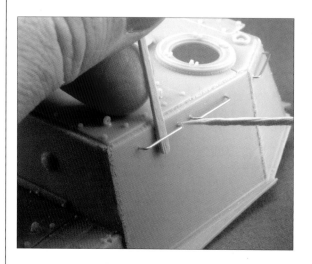

This final step consists of attaching the grab handle to the plastic hull with superglue. I used toothpicks to maintain the proper distance between the hull area and the brass grab handle.

After supergluing the brass grab handles, a small drop of Mr Surfacer 1000 is applied to seal and even out the area. When dry, a quick sanding with Tamiya fine sandpaper removes any uneven areas around each grab handle. Remember not to sand too closely, as these grab handles were welded on. Leave a slight overflow of some 'cast texture' to give the impression of welding.

I added pock-mark texture to the back plate using a small dental bit in my Dremel drill. Without adding pressure, let the weight of the Dremel drill flow randomly over the required area.

Afterwards, lightly sand the area and if necessary redo the area until satisfied. It is easy to go overboard with this: subtlety is the key.

The tracks

The Dragon kit's individual link-to-link tracks are nicely moulded and pretty accurate to boot. The only problem area is the two ejector marks on the inside of each link.

Glueing the tracks can be somewhat daunting; however, the photos here show some easy steps that may help out. Make sure the open or unattached end lies at the middle bottom of the vehicle: this will make things easier when removing the tracks for re-fitting after painting. When you are ready to permanently set the tracks, 'Q-tip' or cotton-bud heads are perfect for setting the track sag. Be sure to apply a quick coat of Tamiya extra-thin glue onto the track, as this will help solidify the setting of the track overnight.

After a night of drying out, you should gently and carefully remove the tracks from the kit. As an extra precaution, don't glue any of the wheels or return rollers in place at this time. You'll find that you might need to take one or two off when attaching or reattaching the tracks. When the tracks are stiff and dry, a quick stippled coat of Mr Surfacer 500 on the insides will seal this area and cover up some of the horrible ejector marks.

Detaching the individual tracks is easy using straight-edged nail clippers.

The main aim when attaching together these link-to-link non-workable tracks is to keep them in line and very straight. Make sure that they aren't too tight and that there is ample space to wrap them around the rear drive sprocket.

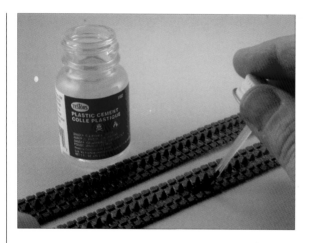

Testors' slow-drying glue is perfect for this application, giving ample time for installation on the vehicle and keeping the tracks workable. After assembling about 20 tracks, give them a quick coat of the glue – just enough to thinly coat the tracks.

While still wet and movable, place one track set onto the kit, making sure the tracks go in the right direction.

A view of the front area shows how menacing the vehicle looks without its front fenders.

From this top view it's easy to see that little detailing was required. Building this kit out of the box is a breeze.

Multiple thin coats of Tamiya Dark Green XF-61 were sprayed, with the addition of Tamiya XF-2 Flat White to fade the tone.

When in position, the Eduard mask was misted with Tamiya Flat White, although it wasn't done too cleanly! However, given the precision of my Iwata Custom Micron, simple touch-ups of the base coat Tamiya Dark Green would not be a problem to do.

Because this was a winter-wash vehicle, I lightly sprayed a cloud-like misty coat of Tamiya XF-2 Flat White on to the panels, usually starting from the centre of an area and working outwards. I knew I wanted a really faded look to the kit and I wasn't too worried about the markings.

After a day or two of drying, the tracks can be prepared for painting. Since they are already dark in colour, a quick coat of Tamiya XF-69 Nato Black is all that is required. Weathering the tracks was easy, and completed in a similar way to the Tamiya thinner/pastel mud process applied to the wheel section. I generally like to use only three shades of earth-tone pastel, with additional black and white tones for mixing in. I like the Holbein line of chalk-type pastels, and I find them very easy to use. After an application of a darker pastel tone and some quick dry-brushing of black oils, the tracks are set aside, ready for installation later.

Painting, weathering and markings

I decided early on that I would showcase this kit in a winter-wash type finish. Winter whitewash was a water-based paint, usually applied with great haste, that was painted over the base coat colour of the tanks and vehicles during the winter months of World War II. The harsh winter environment usually meant the white paint wore off, often giving the vehicle a patchy and faded overall look, with the base coat colour often visible.

I firmly believe that the key to successful weathering is to try to focus on how the type of weather and location affects the vehicle. In this case, I wanted to show a vehicle in Russia, late in the war, and during late-winter or early-spring.

Firstly a good coat of Tamiya Nato Black is sprayed all over the vehicle. Tamiya XF-61 Dark Green was my choice for the base coat, although for Russian vehicles any variant of a dark green is acceptable. There was little standardisation of colour, and whatever colour was available was used. I then lightly sprayed a cloud-like misty coat of Tamiya white onto the panels, starting from the centre of any given area and working outwards. The key is to be as subtle as possible.

Markings

Although I didn't base this kit on any specific vehicle or photograph, I did check my references for extra inspiration, especially for the overall faded worn look and to get an idea of historically correct markings. Eduard's Express Masks no. XT 027 was used to spray on the tactical numbers. These masks are great and I cannot recommend them enough, especially considering the fact that I deplore using decals of any sort.

Here is the 'sponge technique' in action. Experimenting with viscosities of paint is important for the right effect. After a secondary coat of white was misted on, I used heavily thinned Tamiya Dark Green XF-61 and applied it with the sponge. As the painting progressed, another sponging of green Tamiya acrylic was applied. A final misting of heavily thinned white sealed the vehicle and gave it a more uniform look.

Step 1: Tamiya XF-69 Nato Black is applied as the base coat, making an even backing for the base colours.

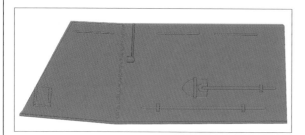

Step 2: Tamiya Dark Green XF-61 is applied in thin, even coats, letting some of the black base coat show, especially in corners and at edges.

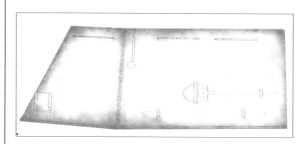

Step 4: Dip your sponge (I use a make-up applicator) in thinned Tamiya Dark Green XF-61, and dab out the excess on a scrap piece of paper until it has a 'workable' coating. Then dab the paint on, which should give you an instant 'chipped' effect. Practise on an old model first, and you'll get the hang of it after a while.

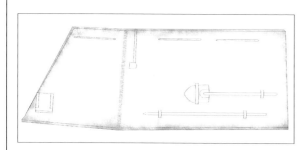

Step 6: Repeat the sponge application, but not as much as the first time. With different layers of paint, the shades start working, especially when another, lighter misting of flat white is applied.

The 'sponge technique'

After the markings had been added, I applied my 'sponge technique' – something I've seen before in other artistic applications but have never applied to modelling per se. The winter-wash scheme is something I'm constantly experimenting with, and so this seemed like a good occasion to try it out. In short, it is applied by 'dabbing', much like stippling, and requires a little practice to achieve a good result. Once again, I tried to execute this as subtly as possible.

Adjusting the viscosity of paint is vital for the right effect too. I've done this for most of the models in this

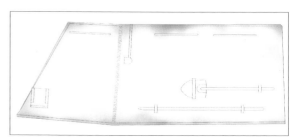

Step 3: A thin coating of Tamiya Flat White is sprayed in very light layers, keeping the green base coat just visible – allowing the forthcoming sponged-on paint colour (which is the same as the base coat) to blend in properly.

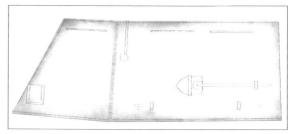

Step 5: Although it may look rather over the top with huge chippings everywhere, just apply another coating of the Tamiya Flat White and you'll see everything tone down.

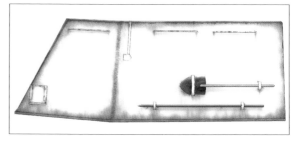

Step 7: Once you are happy with the results, a post-shade and/or several oil washes will make the winter wash stand out. Streaking and chipping can be applied if necessary.

The tracks and front hull are being shaded with Tamiya thinner mixed with some black pastel chalk powder.

One of many washes that were applied to the model kit, to even out the brightness of the paint.

book, except the Cromwell ISU-152, and it's a favoured technique of mine. The accompanying pictures on page 14, created by my good friend and fine illustrator Dan Oldfield, show some general step-by-step instructions for how to achieve the right finish. The key word here though is, inevitably, experimentation. I painted up the smaller items (such as the shovel) with Citadel Colour acrylic paints, from the Games Workshop line. These are some of the best paints for small items, especially tools.

Final weathering

When I was satisfied with the final look I applied a number of washes of Winsor & Newton Ivory Black and Burnt Umber oils, mixed in a ratio of 70:30. The subtle streaks and fading were done with my Iwata Custom Micron and a heavily thinned post-shade mix of Tamiya Flat Black and Tamiya XF-64 Red Brown acrylic paints. Due to the subtlety of the white-wash effect, any additional pastel streaking and fading would detract from its impact. The mud and dust were applied using a dark pastel shade using the 'Tamiya thinner' technique though.

In conclusion, I can safely say that although the Dragon ISU-152 has a few minor problem areas, with a little patience and experimentation with some new painting techniques, you can add new life to this already popular kit.

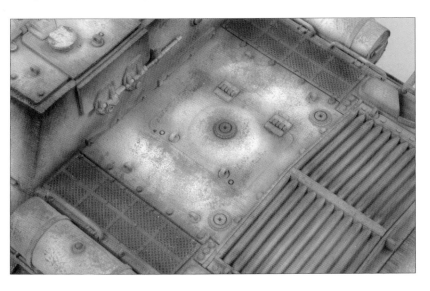

LEFT AND PAGES 16–17: The finished ISU-152 in detail.

Building the IS-2 in 1/35

Subject:	IS-2
Model by:	Nicola Cortese
Skill level:	Master
Kit:	DML JS-2 Stalin II, kit no. 6012
Additional detailing sets used:	1/35 V-2 Engine from Maquette no. 35024
	Modelkasten SK-14 'split-type' workable tracks
	Jordi Rubio replacement metal barrel no. TG-20
	K&S Metal foil sheet for the fenders
	Sheets of 0.05, 0.10 and 0.20 Evergreen styrene and rod
	Tichy Train Groups various eyelet, nut and bolt details
	Athabasca brass-etch eyebolts and liftrings
	Aber photo-etch tie downs no. 35 A95
	Eduard photo-etch set no. 35 194
	Jaguar model JS-II resin interior no. 63501
	Detail Associates brass wire
Markings:	Eduard Express Masks no. XT 027
Paints:	Tamiya XF-13 JA Green
	Tamiya XF-20 Medium Grey
	Tamiya XF-52 Flat Earth
	Tamiya XF-61 Dark Green
	Tamiya XF-69 Nato Black

In recent years, photos of destroyed or damaged vehicles have provided a rich source of inspiration for modellers. Given the amount of detail involved in recreating such subjects, a highly realistic approach to modelling is essential, particularly in terms of modification. It is important to note that removing detail can be just as difficult as adding it, especially when having to open up areas like hatches and engine bays. This chapter will focus on the more advanced skills and attention required in doing this.

The DML/Dragon JS-2 kit first hit the hobbystore shelves in the early 1990s, and has established itself as a favourite modelling subject. Crisp detailing and the generally 'spot-on' dimensions throughout have made this kit one of the manufacturer's most enduring.

I initially thought about presenting this model in a destroyed state, but changed my mind to show it as an abandoned vehicle. The latter would provide better scope for a demonstration of comprehensive modelling techniques, whilst the former would only mean that everything would get lost in the rubble! In addition, one particular double-page spread in *Ground Power* issue 76 (pages 58–59), showing a damaged and abandoned early IS-2, inspired me to use it as a basis for this model. This was an extensive build that involved major reworking, and numerous additional items.

General construction

As was the case for the ISU-152, the lower hull needs to be raised by about 2mm (see pages 7–8). Among the first things that caught my eye when studying the *Ground Power* reference photos was that the vehicle shown was missing its first two return rollers. I decided that this was something I just had to recreate: I did this by

Small details like this often have a big impact on the finished model.

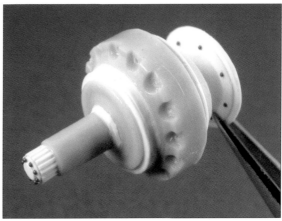

I recreated a detached drive sprocket mechanism by studying one specific photo. Although maybe not 100 per cent accurate, I felt that it looked acceptable.

simply and carefully removing the moulded-in return rollers from the lower hull with the help of a razor saw.

Only three bolts per side were drilled out, as per the real vehicle, even though the return roller has 12 bolt inserts. I presume that this was due to the rationing of parts during this hectic wartime period, it being important to avoid waste and to only use what was necessary.

The interior

Jaguar's resin interior is well done in terms of the moulding, although the instructions are rather vague, and at some point the instruction sheet should be revised. The driver's compartment, partcularly the seat, is a nice piece of work.

The upper hull

In order to display the engine hatch and transmission bay open, a little surgery and an extra donor IS-2 kit were required. The first thing to be done after

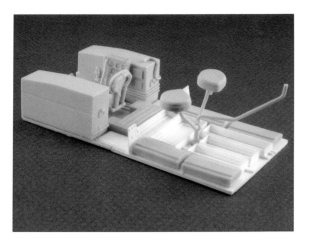

Jaguar's interior is good, although, as you can see by the white styrene, I opted to scratch-build part of the floor interior with styrene to open up the bin containers.

The floor and driver's compartment have been painted and are awaiting weathering. I added a makeshift tarp using a chocolate wrapper. Even though these details won't be seen, at least *I* know they are there!

removing the engine hatches was to open the exhaust grills and to 'box-in' the enclosed open area with 0.10 sheet styrene. I wanted to display one of the exhaust grills in an open position so that the ribbing of the exhaust bay could be seen.

Eduard's excellent photo-etch grills were a perfect fit, although I had to fabricate the three tiny exhaust hinges with 0.10 brass rod. I removed the louvres from the rear deck exhaust and replaced them with Plastruct 0.10 x 0.80 styrene strip, which I measured and cut with my 'Chopper' cutting board. I added a little more verism by detaching some of them from the frames, as this was common in many of the photos I'd seen, and included Tichy Train Groups eyelets to replace the liftrings.

The engine and drive train

I opted to use Maquette's plastic T-34 V-2 engine kit as the basis for the engine and drive train, figuring it would be an acceptable platform to replicate an IS-2 engine and drive train.

The most intriguing part of the DML kit is the cooling fan, which is moulded as a solid object. Given the exposed engine detail, I decided to scratch-build the item, using the kit's cooling fan as a rough template. The fan filter was fabricated from styrene sheet, following careful examination of key reference photos. Note that it is extremely difficult to find specific shots of engine interiors, and as a result measuring up and trying to get the final look just right can be a challenging prospect. I used my Staedtler combo circle template to make a circular template for one part of the fan – this is a technique that can be used to make all kinds of small rings and discs. I then drilled out the inner part with my Dremel, and cut round the outer edge with scissors, finishing off with a light sanding to even out the edges.

Because I wanted to display the transmission, I really had to improve the Maquette plastic offering. After studying the limited number of available photos, I based the final transmission on Maquette's part, which is rather simplified but still acceptable. The transmission is a simple, two-piece affair, which, with a little help from

BELOW The rear deck in the preliminary stages. Once the moulded-in exhaust grills had been removed, I 'boxed in' the enclosed open area with 0.10 sheet styrene.

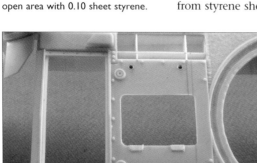

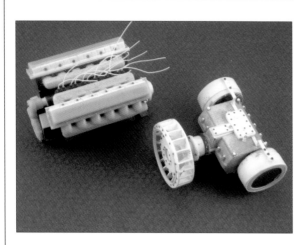

Maquette's plastic T-34 engine and transmission is a rather basic offering, but with some scratch-building and minor tweaks, it can be brought up to acceptable standards.

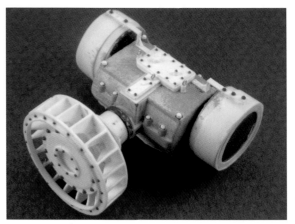

Hours of detailing went into replicating the transmission and cooling fan, mainly working with a couple of photos. After sanding off the top portion, I removed the moulded-in bolt detail, which I later replaced with various bolts fashioned by my Historex punch set. Tichy Train Groups came to the rescue once more with some small 0.20 rivets and nuts and bolts.

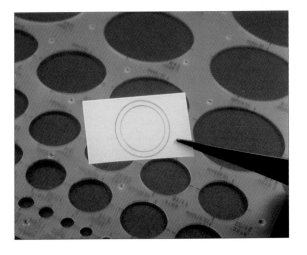

This photo shows how to make a small ring or disc. As you can see a smaller inner circle has been added to a larger outer one.

Made specifically for train modellers, Athabasca's brass-etch eyebolts and liftrings were a perfect match when it was time to detail up the transmission.

some styrene, Historex nut and bolt detail and the extremely tiny Athabasca eyelets and Tichy Train Groups 0.20 rivets, can be much improved. I purchased two of these kits (the other was for the IS-3 build) – and, with my customary luck, I found that they came in two different colours, black and light grey! Ever the optimist, I decided to mix up the two kits when building, just to give an interesting look to the final product.

The engine 'plumbing' was created with Plastruct 0.10 rod, and bolt detail was from Tichy Train Groups' 'Nut and Bolt' set. I fabricated (what seems to be) the engine air filter from stacked styrene discs and added a brass disc from my spares box.

Building the engine bay

Building the engine bay was quite a challenge, mainly due to the lack of clear and precise reference material. I painstakingly fabricated the interior engine bay with lots of different-sized styrene sheets and U-Beam strips. Personally, I find this the most fun and rewarding part of the whole scratch-building process. The fact that with restricted reference material you can create an acceptable (albeit not perfect) replica is highly rewarding. It definitely helped hone my scratch-building skills too!

The turret

After much deliberation, I decided to use the kit turret as a platform to display some more scratch-building and to add some of the Jaguar bits.

I replaced the kit's plastic grab handles with 0.19 brass wire. In early IS-2s, the top grab handles are slightly off-centre. Having attached the grab handles with superglue I went back and trimmed the brass from the inside of the turret, because of the small interior bits to be added there afterwards. I also added a quick coat of Mr Surfacer 1000 to the inner walls of the turret to smooth out the area for the interior parts. I continued to add a mixture of Jaguar and scratch-built items here too. Even though most of this work won't be visible in the end, it's nice to know it's there.

Scratch-building both the commander's and driver's hatches were mini projects in themselves, and the final results were very satisfying: I didn't feel that Dragon's hatches were up to standard. The most difficult part was achieving a realistic look for the outer lip: the real hatches are semi-oval in shape. I enjoyed replicating the periscope detail too.

I cautiously improvised as I went along, adding bolt and nut detail, constantly referring to reference photos. It took much dry-fitting and measuring up to get the transmission right.

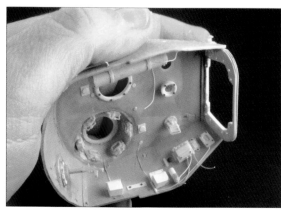

After deciding not to use Jaguar's resin turret, I scratch-built the various interior items with styrene strip and rod.

I added the Jaguar commander's cupola to the kit turret mainly because of the nicely cast texture and the inclusion of the inner periscopes. This was fairly easy to do, although the top part of the kit had to be widened slightly so that the cupola could sit properly. The interior of the turret was painted and weathered.

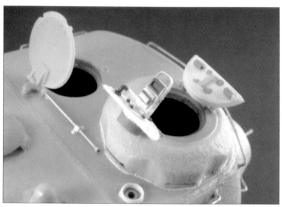

The commander's hatch was a mix of styrene strip, and aftermarket nut and bolt detail. Part of the periscope comes from the Tamiya IS-3 kit.

Aber photo-etch tie downs were used for the handles for the driver's hatch. A thin piece of Tamiya tape was used to simulate the strap handle.

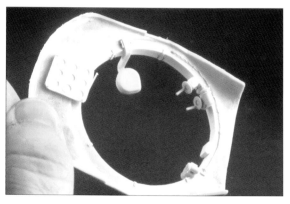

Some of Jaguar's resin items were used in the bottom half of the turret assembly, though I scratch-built most of the items. When everything is together, it's quite a 'tight fit' – just like the real vehicle.

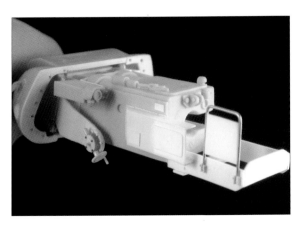

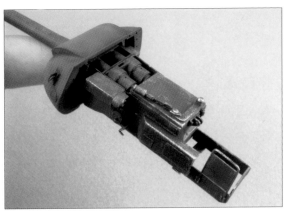

There are some major details missing from the gun cradle and lifting mechanism, so I scratch-built these items. Some of the resin parts were so badly warped too that it was easier to craft styrene replacements.

A view of the painted gun. Semi-gloss black seemed like the right colour to me.

The gun

Jordi Rubio's barrels make a nice addition to any model, although the DML gun moulding and detail is good. I replaced and added detail with styrene sheet to areas I thought could be improved, such as the front mantlet cover. One of my reference photos in particular intrigued me: it showed the mantlet detached from the turret, and also that the mantlet holding ring was in two pieces. So, I carefully separated the kit's one-piece item with a razor saw, keeping it damp with warm water to reduce styrene dust.

The tracks

The IS-2, and the entire range of Stalin tanks, featured 'split links', which were regular links with every other guide tooth missing. They were used to keep weight down to a minimum. I decided to use Modelkasten replacement tracks for this project. Manufactured in Japan, their workable and non-workable tracks are among the best plastic ones available. As explained in the previous chapter, a liberal coating of Tamiya's Nato Black was applied to seal and coat

I slowly took my time to get an even, straight cut when separating the one-piece mantlet.

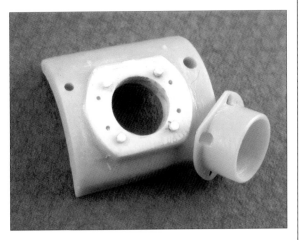

Once separated, I added a styrene backing to the mantlet and four bolts that are connected to it. The mantlet holding ring needed some fine drilling and sanding to remove the unwanted plastic.

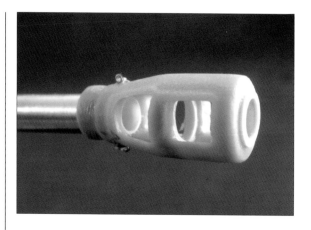

A close-up photo revealing the detail added to the gun muzzle break, including the tiny photo-etch lifting lugs from Athabasca, brass-etch eyebolts and Historex-punched discs. I also added styrene to the inner portion and made a new front 'ring'.

Modelkasten early split-link tracks were my first choice as a replacement for this particular model. Unfortunately, these are marred by two 'knock-out' marks on each track link.

A couple of quick stippled coats of Mr Surfacer 1000 can cover the 'knock-out' marks – better than sanding every track individually!

As per my usual routine, I applied a darker pastel tone and a quick dry-brushing of black oils, before leaving aside the tracks for installation later.

the tracks prior to a quick application of dark earth pastels – very much my standard procedure!

Creating a simple display base

I wanted to display my finished model on a small diorama-type base. Instead of scratch-building one, I decided to try the Trakz TX 0018 AFV Diorama Base, which is made from lightweight polyvinyl.

Painting it up was simple, and I used a mixture of Tamiya acrylics. I started with a base coat of Tamiya XF-69 Nato Black, and then airbrushed it with various shades of XF-52 Flat Earth and XF-61 Dark Green, coating it with heavily thinned layers of paint.

Painting and weathering

Before beginning to paint the model, I had to picture the vehicle in my mind's eye, sitting abandoned, with hatches open, parts missing and the mantlet detached. This would have an important effect on the selected finish.

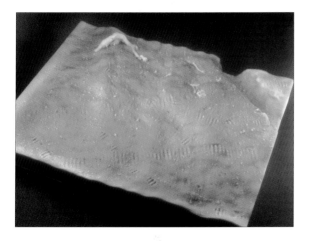

The gravel-like texture of the base is perfect for what I was looking for – barren, rough terrain.

I finished off painting the base with a light misting of Buff colour, giving it a dusty look.

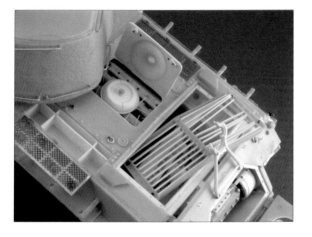

A top view of the rear deck before painting commences. How the parts are placed is vital to the final overall presentation.

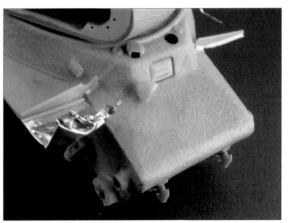

To add to the overall realism, I formed a mangled front fender from K&S Metal foil sheet, which worked really well. K&S Metal is available in rolls and each one will last a long time.

Tamiya JA Green XF-13 was chosen for the base colour. This is a nice rich colour that I've used before, and which I know works well in conjunction with a lighter weathering colour.

A pre-shading layer of Tamiya Nato Black XF-69 was first sprayed over the entire kit. Next, the painting proper began (as always) with thin layers of shaded colour, starting off with the 'out of the bottle' colour before adding on lighter shades until I felt the look was just right. Since this vehicle was supposed to be an abandoned and dusty one, I wanted to add some sort of weathering, and to do this I used the 'sponge technique' described previously. I dabbed the model with a very subtle post-shade mix of Tamiya paint, which is barely visible yet works well.

At this point, the weathering is not too heavy still, and markings can be applied. I chose Eduard's excellent Express Masks no. XT 027, which are easy to use and merely require you to spray on the right colour. After placing the mask on the turret I misted on a couple of coats of Tamiya Flat White until I was happy with the results. Next I sprayed on a post-shade mix of Tamiya Flat Black and Tamiya Red Brown acrylics in a ratio of 4:1, carefully adding this where oil washes would normally go, with the aim of enhancing with paint rather than

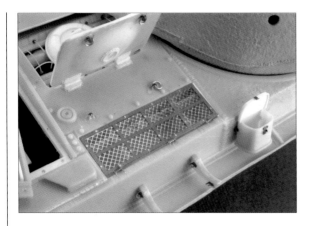

Eduard photo-etch set 35194 was partially used for the exhaust screens and mostly smaller items. In this pre-painting photo the etch screens have merely been placed on, because when the pre-shading starts you don't want to be spending time spraying paint though those screens. I also partially scratch-built the engine hatch cover and mounts.

Getting everything to line up was the hardest part of the rear engine deck. In many photos I've seen of vehicles in this state, the rear back plate is often hanging off or completely missing, so I positioned it so that the left side was detached and was just held on by two bolts.

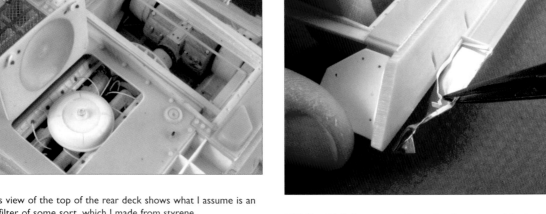

This view of the top of the rear deck shows what I assume is an air filter of some sort, which I made from styrene.

BELOW I also decided to scratch-build the inner workings of one of the road wheels.

K&S Metal foil sheet was again used to form part of the back fender. To add to the realism I cut pieces of 0.05 styrene strips to replicate the metal strips that attach the fenders to the hull.

with oils. Next a number of washes were applied to even out the contrast in the model's colour. I then mixed some dark pastels into the post-shade mix and once more used the sponge to apply them. This produced the encrusted, slightly dirty appearance I was looking to achieve.

All that remained to be done was to add the final weathering touches, comprising a little light streaking with oil paints to represent rust and dirt marks.

Perfecting the look of a vehicle that has been out in the elements for some time was difficult, and this was by no means a weekend project. However, I feel the project was a good learning experience for me and I enjoyed the challenge of mixing up scratch-building techniques, and resin and photo-etch parts.

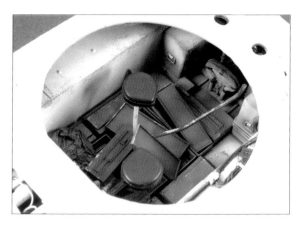

The interior of the turret and gun, painted and weathered and awaiting installation – although it will be hardly noticed! Note the chipping effects in and around the sides and corners.

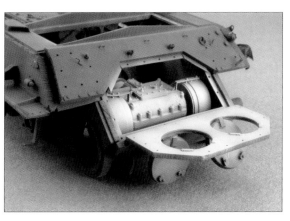

After a little research, I decided on Tamiya XF-20 Medium Grey for the engine bay area, which I thought would contrast nicely with the rich green hull colour. At this point everything was in sub-assembly stage except for the tracks, which have already been painted and weathered up.

Turret number '222' was chosen from Eduard's excellent Express Masks XT 027. I misted on a couple of coats of Tamiya Flat White to get a nice clean result.

More of the 'sponge technique' was carried out, using heavily thinned Tamiya XF-69 Nato Black.

I weathered the turret with various layers of paint and shades to achieve a really worn look.

The weathering process in its opening stages.

I added a layer of caked-on mud to the underside and lower hull using medium-shade pastels and Tamiya thinner.

An easy way to paint the metal wheels is to simply dab a small amount of paint on a cloth and wipe it on. The paint is a Citadel Colour acrylic called Chain Mail.

Applying light rust streaks throughout with oil paint should be done as subtlly as possible. Burnt Umber mixed super thin was applied with a clean brush.

Prismicolour pencil was used to add a very faint hint of metal.

ABOVE AND PAGES 30–31: The finished IS-2 installed on its base.

Building the IS-3M in 1/35

Subject:	IS-3M
Model by:	Nicola Cortese
Skill level:	Advanced
Kit:	Trumpeter JS-3M Kit no. 316
Additional detailing sets used:	Armour Track Models plastic workable replacement tracks no. TK-12
	Tichy Train Groups various eyelet, nut and bolt details
	Sheets and strips of 0.05, 0.10 and 0.20
	Evergreen styrene, and various sizes of styrene rod
Paints:	Tamiya XF-13 JA Green
	Tamiya XF-57 Buff
	Tamiya XF-69 Nato Black

Trumpeter's IS-3M really caught my eye when it first came out in 2002. It's a kit that calls out for more advanced scratch-building, upgrade and detailing techniques. At first inspection, it looks like a close copy of Tamiya's excellent IS-3 kit, with the same sprue layout and overall style. It comprises 224 parts of soft but very workable dark olive drab plastic. In no way is it as crisp and well defined as the Tamiya offering, but it is perfectly acceptable nonetheless.

I had always wanted to build a post-war variant of this vehicle, especially in a desert paint scheme. Considering that virtually all of the Russian vehicles were painted in dark green it was a real breath of fresh air to have alternate paint scheme to choose from, especially the Egyptian 'sand' colour. Some good starting points for those who would like to familiarise themselves with the vehicle are Rossagraph's concise *Model Detail* no. 7, and issue 77 of the excellent Japanese publication *Ground Power*.

Preparations

As per normal, I soaked the sprues in warm soapy water before getting work underway, and rinsed them in cold water before letting the trees dry overnight. Trumpeter plastic seems to adhere together so much better when some of the excess plastic mould-release residue is washed off.

When building the upper hull, be careful to make sure the sides line up with the separate side skirts. If they don't, you will end up with unsightly gaps. Other than that, the kit is quite easy to build with no major problems to look out for. Below are some other points to take note of when building the Trumpeter JS-3M kit.

The front glacis

I scraped off all the unwanted raised detail on the front glacis, such as the moulded-on wire detail for the headlights. Because I wanted to scratch-build various new items, I filled in some areas to create a nice, clean build area to work on, using pieces of styrene rod. After drying, a quick snip of the cutters and a sanding is all that is needed.

I felt that the front glacis's welded appearance left much to be desired, and I especially wanted to enhance the front bottom plate welds. With help from my Dremel and a dental bit, I proceeded to form a new opening, into which I would place cut and measured strips of styrene 0.10 rod. These were dabbed

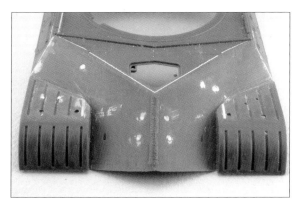

The front hull surface has been filled, scraped and sanded, ready for some scratch-built extras.

The kit's front glacis weld seams left much to be desired, so with my Dremel I carved out a thin opening for some new welds made from styrene 0.10 rod.

with glue, and then marks were cut into the still-wet glue to produce a better weld effect. I added cast texture by applying coats of Mr Surfacer 500 to the entire front area. I use Mr. Surfacer primarily for filling in tiny holes and gaps (using a toothpick) or for adding texturing (using a nylon brush): it is easy to sand smooth too, and does not leave a grainy residue. I stippled it on with a closely cropped nylon brush. I applied several coats of the thinner Mr Surfacer 1000, again using the nylon brush. It took a couple of applications to get the nice cast texture I was looking for, and I let each coat dry for about 10 minutes before adding another layer.

To clean the nylon brush after use, dip it in a jar of Testors thinners, which will remove the excess liquid, and dry it off with a paper towel. I've been using the same brush for a couple of years now and with proper care it will no doubt be usable for many years to come. Afterwards I started building up the front area, adding the massive tow hooks and spring-loaded retainers from the spares box (I managed to scrape off the kit's poor representations).

The upper hull

Trumpeter neglected to add smaller, subtle details such as the torch-cut metal parts, so prominent throughout these vehicles. These ran right across the vehicles'

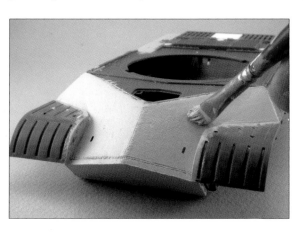

A nice cast texture was created using Mr Surfacer 500, applied with a nylon brush, followed by a light sanding when dry.

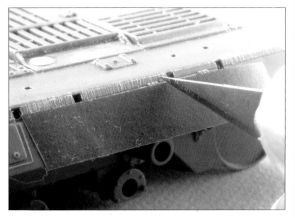

I replicated the torch-cut metal on the superstructure sides by carefully carving into the plastic with an Xacto knife, then adding a quick coat of Tamiya super fine glue to seal the welds together and make them more uniform.

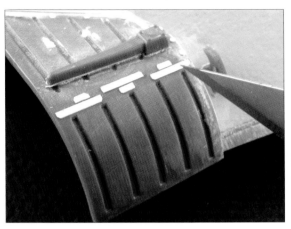

I went the 'extra step' with the engine-deck detail, carefully removing the area with my Dremel drill and cautiously sanding to the correct size. I then measured, cut and glued a piece of 0.20 styrene sheet to replicate the deck portion.

The hinge attachments are made from 0.05 styrene strips, carefully measured, cut and glued into position.

superstructures and are quite distinctive. The side guards for the turret ring also needed attention, as they sit way to low – so low, in fact, that they seem to be welded to the side bin! I filled in the open portion where the ring should be with styrene strip, and raised the guard to an acceptable level. After checking scale plans in various publications, I noted that Trumpeter had made the same mistake as Tamiya on the rear engine deck, with part of it being too narrow. I decided to correct this in my build.

The fuel tanks are nicely done, but, ever ready for a challenge, I added grab handles made with 0.05 sheet strips cut to size. I carefully bent the small thin strip into sections with pliers then added a small drop of Tamiya Extra Thin glue to set them into place. As I was researching, I discovered a few more details on the fuel tanks, such as bolt detail and the drainage plug right underneath the fuel tank itself, so I added these too.

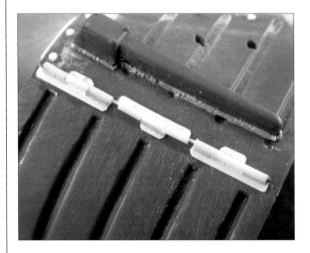

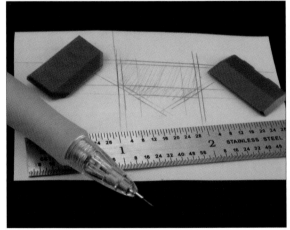

To get the hinged effect just right, 0.20 styrene rod was cut into three equal pieces to make up the actual mechanism. Thin pieces of stretched sprue were used for the tiny wire between each hinge. A 0.20 bolt was added to each end. I replicated the tiny welds that attach the hinges to the fender with very thin stretched sprue.

Here's how I replaced the mantlet. Firstly, I measured and copied the dimensions of the Tamiya mantlet cover onto a 0.10 sheet of styrene.

I also felt the front and back fenders, specifically the hinge detail on the front fenders, needed extra attention. Trumpeter's offerings look too bland and 'toy-like' for my taste – although I would challenge myself to detail these items to an acceptable level.

After replacing the lifting rings on the back engine deck I concentrated on adding small details like fuel lines and bolt detail, and generally enhancing the appearance as much as possible.

The turret

Trumpeter seemed to have gotten the turret cast texture spot on: however, the kit-supplied turret grab handles and rails are pretty thick and don't line up properly with the indicated holes. No big drama: I applied a dab of Tamiya putty on the top and attached the grab handles in the bottom attachment points. Cast texture was missing from the muzzle brake; however, I've seen some IS-3Ms with heavy texture and others with minimal texture. I added a light cast texture with Mr Surfacer 1000, creating a nice contrast.

The D-25T gun barrel is a two-piece affair and is not perfectly round, but with some help from a Squadron Tri-Grit sanding stick it was sanded straight

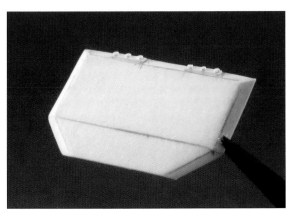

I carefully cut the sides, lined up the edges with pliers, and then added a dab of Tamiya Extra Thin cement to the inside for extra strength.

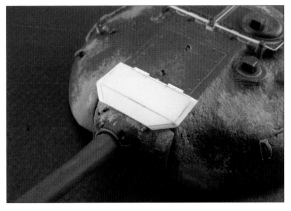

It took about an hour to do this piece, and although not perfect, it looked far better than the kit-supplied item.

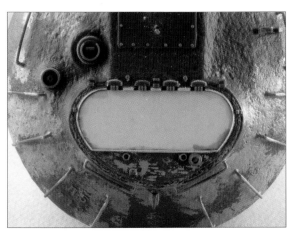

I filled in this area with styrene card and added the proper border height with styrene strip and the welds all around.

Substituting the kit torsion bars for the hatches required more than just replacing them with 0.10 styrene rod. To get a straight, even height the small middle mount had to be raised slightly.

and smooth. After adding some small bolt and etch detail to the muzzle break, I tried to simulate 'mould shift' casting by adding styrene rod in small sections: although hardly noticeable, it's one of those subtle touches that makes the finished product more appealing.

Surprisingly, Trumpeter (and Tamiya) omitted the two obvious lifting rings from the gun mantlet: I replaced these with Tichy Train Groups plastic eyebolts. I also replaced the two on the turret top plate with the same, as these too are rather bland. The kit-supplied mantlet cover lacked sufficient resemblance to the actual item, so I decided to scratch-build a new item using the Tamiya mantlet cover as a template.

The turret hatches were also a poor fit, with large gaps on either side, and they lacked a proper border. The torsion bar along the front of the hatches should be two thinner items. I glued the kit torsion bar to the kit, removed the moulded bar, then carefully replaced it with 0.10 styrene rod.

I replaced the lower back-turret rain flashing with two pieces of styrene, which looked much better than the kit-supplied item. The 12.7mm DShKM anti-aircraft machine gun is not as crisp as Tamiya's, but with some bolts and styrene bits added it looked presentable.

The tracks

The kit-supplied rubber tracks are acceptable, mainly because the hanging side fenders mean you can only partially see them. However, I recently received a set of Armour Track Model TK-12 tracks and couldn't wait to try them on this model. These tracks are well worth the money! They are reminiscent of Modelkasten's work, and are crisp and well moulded throughout, with no knockout marks to be seen. The cutting and cleaning was done in less than two hours.

When it came to painting the tracks, once more Tamiya Nato Black was used, and I made sure to get in-between the track links.

Painting and weathering

Since getting into the hobby, I've been very lucky to meet some of the finest modellers, who have always been gracious with their time in helping me out. I'm continuously experimenting with different painting and weathering techniques and frankly, for me, I find the least amount of finishing steps to be the most rewarding – there are fewer chances to make mistakes. This particular

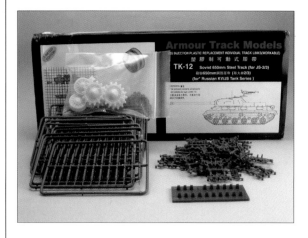

Armour Track Models 'workable' plastic tracks are a great replacement for the JS-3M kit's vinyl offering. Resin drive sprockets and a set of idler wheels are also included, as is a plastic jig to help with track assembly.

Holbein's chalk-type pastels sticks are my favourite. I only work with three different tones of earthen pastels with additional black and white tones for the mixing. Using a Dremel drill with a coarse bit reduces the pastel sticks to a fine powdered state in a matter of minutes.

After an application of the darker pastels using the Tamiya thinner method, I brushed on some lighter pastels to add more dimension. There are no set rules here; whatever looks good and works for you is key.

Brushing Tamiya thinner mixed with black pastel powder to the middle area of the track added depth.

A close view of the front plate area shows what can be done with styrene and detailed reference material. The headlight wiring was made from 0.10 styrene rod and the back of the horn was partially scratch-built with punched discs.

This view shows the test fitting of the tracks and the side skirts.

Note that part of the engine deck area has been coated with Mr Surfacer 500 to add texture.

The many tiny turret tie downs were made from pieces of stretched sprue and bent to shape with the help of the tip of my pliers.

I came to the conclusion that a special mix of Tamiya Buff and Flat White would recreate the specific desert colour I was looking for.

paint scheme is like a winter wash coat in many ways – darker base coat, then a lighter coat, with various degrees of paint chipping and fading. A vehicle that has been in the desert in all the elements can be a difficult one to bring to life, considering its monotone base colour.

Pre-shading coat

I executed my usual pre-shading of Tamiya XF-69 Nato Black over the model. Because of the contrast between the white styrene and the dark green of the plastic, I was careful to ensure that the pending base coat colours had an even palette to work on. I always used to leave unsightly fingerprints on my wet models, so now I take extra care when handling them at this stage: I invested in a box of latex gloves. Needless to say my wife was somewhat surprised and concerned upon first hearing the snapping and stretching from my modelling room when I first struggled to get them on!

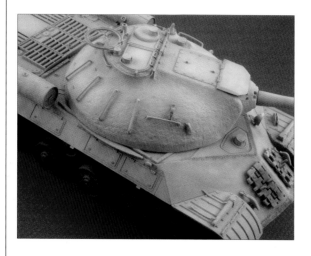

I carefully built up lighter layers of the Tamiya XF-57 Buff colour.

A light misting of Tamiya XF-57 Buff both tones down the contrast and brings out the sponge effect at the same time.

This photo shows how a light wash with oils can bring out the finest of features.

Another thin coating of the Tamiya XF-13 JA Green was sponged on, prior to another, even thinner base coat of Tamiya XF-57 Buff. Once satisfied with the overall look, it was time to apply a post-shade of Tamiya XF-1 Flat Black and Tamiya XF-64 Red Brown acrylic paints, to bring out some much needed contrast.

The base coat

From what I can surmise, the actual base colour was pale sand, almost white, and it had some of the original Russian green paint still visible underneath. I took the same approach to applying the paint with a sponge as I did with the DML ISU-152 build. I carefully built up light layers of Tamiya Buff, normally in central areas.

Mainly because of the high contrast and the overall brightness of the paint scheme, it is easy to overpaint, and for the model to take on a 'cartoon-like' appearance.

I then reapplied thinned Tamiya XF-13 JA Green with a sponge to the various areas where weathering would occur. Although it may look terrible at first and you might get discouraged, rest assured it will look good once you get to the next step. Another couple of subsequent coatings of Tamiya Buff sealed and evened out the sponge application, giving the almost transparent, worn-out look I was hoping for. See the step-by-step illustrations on pages 14–15 for how to achieve this effect.

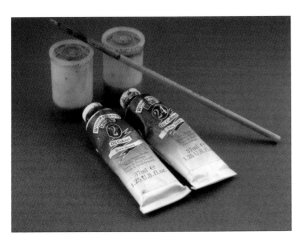

Winsor & Newton Ivory Black and Burnt Umber (70:30) is the usual wash mix I prefer.

The front fender receives the first of many washes. Because of the light paint scheme I wasn't too heavy with the post-shading, preferring to let the washes do the work.

Pastel streaks were applied with a brush and a mix of white and a light earth pastel. It is important not to overdo the streaking, especially with a pale scheme. Knowing how to use the right tones of pastels is also vital.

To replicate the rectangular slits evident on the IS-3's skirts, instead of cutting through out the rather thick, one-piece plastic side skirts of the Trumpeter kit, I decided to just make a template with the help of Tamiya tape. I painted them Tamiya XF-1 Flat Black.

I dabbed a drop of Tamiya thinner mixed with black pastel powder onto the end connectors of the tracks, adding a little depth and contrast.

Minute scratches were created by using a square-tip large brush with a bit of darker pastel on it. It's best to experiment with this before applying it.

The washes

To bring out the contrast of the paint and the weathering effect, a number of subtle washes were applied. Once again Winsor & Newton oil paints were used. A primary coat of heavily thinned Burnt Sienna was applied to small sections at a time. I like semi-transparent film canisters for mixing my oils in because you can judge the quantity and colour better. I generally use odourless solvents to thin out the oils.

Winsor & Newton Ivory Black and Burnt Umber were mixed in a ratio of 70:30 for the final wash itself, with a darker wash on hand if needed. The capillary action of the oil wash in corners and crevices brings the model to life. Excessive washes can be detrimental to the overall finish to a well painted model, so be patient and be careful not to go overboard.

Pastel streaking was also subtlly applied to the finished model, something hard to see unless observing at close quarters. I also added a bit of mud to the front plate, just to give it some light weathering.

Trumpeter's JS-3M was not without detail problems and omissions, even though these were small. Overall, I'm sure many have been contemplating building this kit since it first came out, and frankly I enjoyed it so much I can't wait to build another!

OPPOSITE AND PAGE 42: the completed IS-3M.

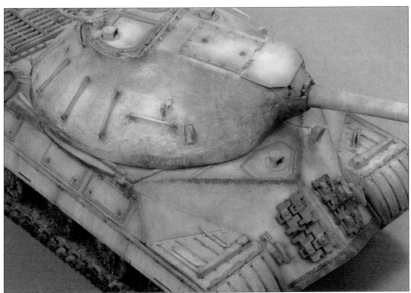

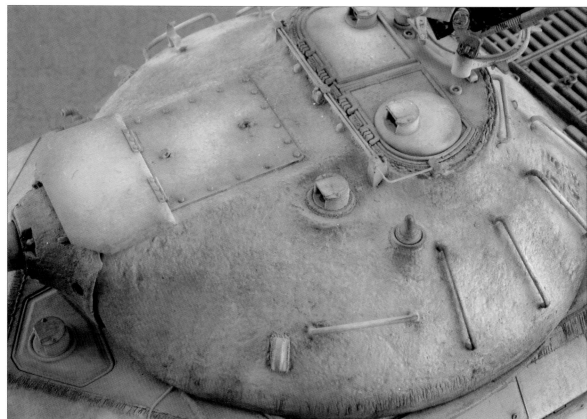

Building the IS-3 in 1/35

Subject:	*IS-3*
Model by:	*Nicola Cortese*
Skill level:	*Master*
Kit:	*Tamiya kit no. 35211, Stalin JS-3 Heavy Tank*
Additional detailing sets used:	*1/35 V-2 Engine from Maquette no. 35024*
	Friulmodel ALT-54 'split-type' workable replacement tracks
	Jordi Rubio replacement metal barrel TG-20
	Aber 35035 IS-3 Stalin etch set
	Tichy Train Groups various eyelet, nut and bolt details
	Sheets of 0.05, 0.10 and 0.20 Evergreen styrene, and rod
	Modelkasten A-4 wingnuts
Markings:	*Eduard Express Masks XT Russian Star sheet*
Paints:	*Tamiya XF-7 Red*
	Tamiya XF-69 Nato Black
	Gunze Sangyo H-73 Dark Green

In this chapter, I'll use Tamiya's stunning JS-3 kit to feature a 'mixed media' construction project with plenty of scratch-building and super-detailing. In my view, the kit's plastic mouldings are flawless, with no flash whatsoever, and the basic kit can be built in a couple of evenings without too much trouble, although it is not without the odd fault. Tamiya's kit was released as an early-production IS-3 model, without too many extra details; however, the aim here is to focus on adding detail and enhancements to the base offering. For measurement and dimension reference, I once again referred to *Ground Power* no. 77, which features 1/35-scale plans, while for general detail I consulted Rossagraph's *Model Detail* no. 7.

Adding Aber's photo-etched brass detail set

When it came to deciding which photo-etch set to add, there was no question in my mind that Aber would be the one to go for. Although I'm not a huge fan of photo-etch, I think this set is just great. It provides everything to bring the kit up to par, yet without making things too complicated. I find that many photo-etch sets have a repetitive, almost redundant quality about them; however, I was really impressed with this one.

Some key highlights

The Sponson box covers: this kit is supposed to be a prototype or a very early production model, but if you are building a post-1945 vehicle you'll need to add the Sponson box covers.

Tow hook retaining clips: these were installed on the pre-1945 vehicle. I didn't like the one-dimensional aspect of Aber's offering, so I found some replacements in my spares box.

Rear smoke canisters: curiously, Tamiya's kit includes the rear canister cradles, but not the canisters. The only replacement or upgrade available other than this set was the unimpressive Jaguar set. The instructions on how to wire detail the fuel tanks are really great, though often these were missing from the actual vehicle.

Scratch-building the side bins was easier than I thought. Having removed the kit's side, I measured and added a replacement made from 0.10 styrene sheet. The bin compartments are separate sections: attaching the Aber photo-etch bin covers will add a nice touch.

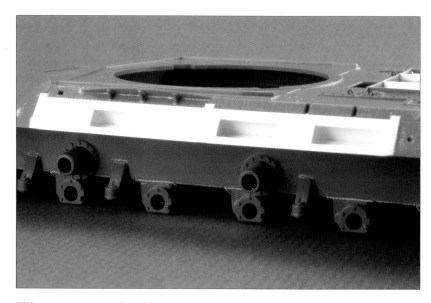

The upper hull

Scratch-building the side bins was not as difficult as I thought. I simply opened up the area carefully by first drilling out the hull sides with my Dremel and then sanding the sides smooth. I replaced the side with 0.10 styrene sheet. Styrene strip ribbing was added to reinforce the inside area.

I measured the bin openings by using the Aber set as a template but then carefully made sure the openings were smaller, as per the real vehicle. Surprisingly, this detailing procedure took a couple of evenings to complete.

Working with Aber photo-etch is pretty easy: it is soft, workable and folds perfectly, plus it adheres to superglue really well. In the accompanying photos, you can see how I replaced the kit's tow shackle mount with the Aber offering.

Tamiya has done a wonderful job of creating texture detail on the front hull section, but I was quite surprised that Tamiya omitted the tow hook retainers from this kit. Aber does supply a photo-etch addition, but I replaced this altogether with DML parts from my spares box. I found the fender texture a little too rough for my liking, considering it is supposed to be sheet metal, and so I lightly sanded these areas to remove it. Aber's set required me to fill in the kit front headlight area: this was easily done with a dab of Tamiya putty and a coating of Mr Surfacer 1000.

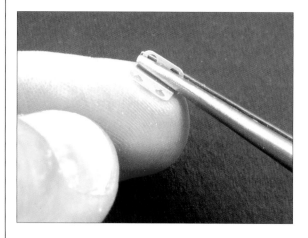

| Aber's photo-etch is easy to bend with just a good pair of pliers.   Ready for installation!

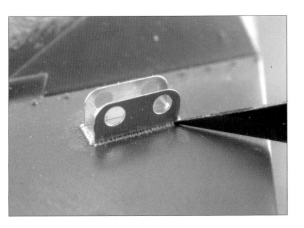

After attaching the tow shackle mount to the front fender, I carefully added a styrene weld seam to the surrounding area.

The tow shackle and tie downs really enhance the front area. Next I added a small dab of Mr Surfacer 1000 around the tiny tie downs, both to improve the final look and to better secure them to the fender.

Rear deck detail

Having checked many photos of the real vehicle, I decided (after much deliberation) to re-do the back engine deck louvres. Tamiya got the rear deck slightly wrong, although this is hardly noticeable. Tamiya has moulded in the rear louvres, but on the real vehicle there appears to be piping going across each section. I carefully measured out the area and cut out the section with my trusty Dremel. Opening up the area is not too difficult, but remember to retain a large enough area to make sanding it smooth easy.

I replaced the rear louvres with Evergreen strip 0.15 x 0.60, but on further inspection perhaps I should have made it a tad thicker to match the scale. For the internal piping, Plastruct 0.20 rod was used. Fabricating this area was quite nerve wracking to say the least. No one ever said scratch-building would be a piece of cake!

Adding engine detail

I don't know why, but lately I seem to have been suffering from a somewhat compulsive desire to open hatches, engines and all manner of compartments on my models. After some careful thought and a bit of planning, I proceeded

I carefully cut out the entire engine louvre compartment, and scratch-built the enclosed compartments with styrene sheet.

Plastruct 0.20 rod was used to replicate the internal piping, and styrene strip was used for the bracing.

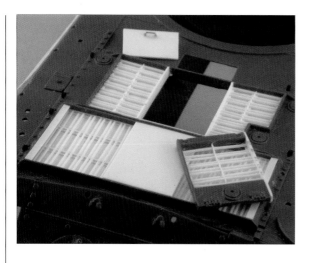

The rear engine deck before adding 0.15 x 0.60 Evergreen strip louvres. Although far from perfect, I felt it was to an acceptable standard. Using my 'Chopper' cutting board made multiple copies a breeze.

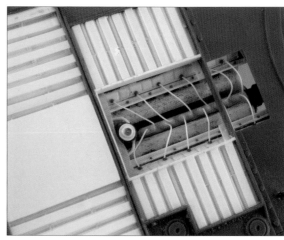

I built the engine fuel nozzle from punched discs and spare parts. Although a pretty basic kit, the Maquette T-34 engine can be built up to acceptable standards. Luckily I found a great reference photo of a real IS-3 engine and hatch detail.

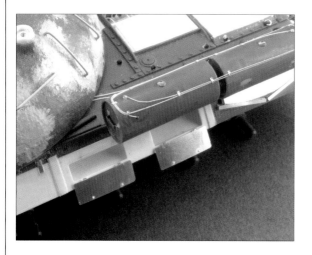

I fabricated fuel lines from some stretched sprue, with brass eyelets for the connection points.

When working on the rear hull, Rossagraph's *Model Detail* no. 7 provided some extremely helpful reference material.

to work out the details and figured out what was achievable. Once again, I used Maquette's plastic V-2 T-34 engine and transmission kit for this area. Luckily, the actual compartment is big enough to take advantage of the engine kit, and the Maquette offering fitted like a glove. I carefully cut out the kit's rear deck, making extra sure not to damage the engine hatch. I added Plastruct 0.20 rod to replicate the internal piping on the hatch: this was built up with styrene strip, and it was quite difficult to get it perfectly aligned. For the wiring, instead of brass or copper wire I used Plastruct 0.10 rod, and bolt detail from Tichy Train Groups Nut and Bolt set. I built up the engine fuel nozzle from punched discs and a perfect brass part (for the nozzle piece) that I found in my spares box.

Tamiya tape was used for what seems to be a protective sheath for the engine. With some minor tweaking, and a careful eye on the references, a pretty good result can be achieved.

Instead of adding both smoke dischargers from the Aber set, I opted to build one and to mangle the other, just to add some extra novelty.

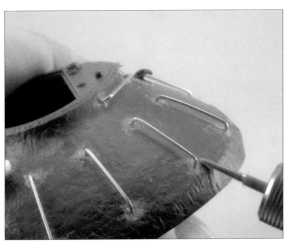

I used my Dremel to smooth out the turret grab handle attachment area with a dental grinding bit.

The antenna mount ring was redone using carefully cut styrene tube.

I used 0.10 brass for the hatch torsion bar mechanism: the tricky part is making sure everything is lined up beforehand.

Improving the fuel tanks

'Dressing up' the fuel tanks was easy to do, and adding bolt detail and photo-etch grab handles really brought these parts to life. The Aber set also includes detailing related to the external fuel cells, for which I used some stretched sprue: I tried using very thin wire but the wire constantly snapped out of place. The fuel-cell grab handles were from the Aber set, and were bent to shape with a pair of nose pliers before being superglued into place.

Replacing the engine lifting rings with Tichy Train Groups eyelets was a welcome upgrade considering the kit's rather bland offerings. I carefully ground down the kit's lifting lugs with my Dremel loaded with a tiny dental bit, and scrapped off the excess with an Xacto blade. Then I drilled out the holes for and inserted the new eyelets.

The turret

Tamiya's IS-3 turret features some stunning cast-iron texture replication. Before integrating any photo-etch onto the turret, I used 0.19 brass rod to replace the

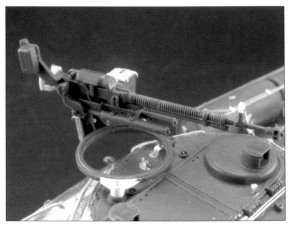

The roof-mounted 12.7mm DShKM machine gun is fantastic. I added Aber's photo-etch pieces but also upgraded both the ammo canister with some added styrene and the machine-gun grab handles with DML's slightly more detailed items.

Another close shot of the 12.7mm DShKM machine gun. I decided to scratch-build the ring-mount roof attachment with discs created by my trusty Historex punch set.

kit's plastic turret grab handles, drilling out the kit's positioning marks and inserting the brass items. A dab of superglue kept the handles in place while a small drop of Mr Surfacer 1000 sealed and uniformed them perfectly.

I decided to scratch-build the antenna mount. Photos show that the mount is in fact a welded ring with an open area for water drainage. First I sanded off all the moulded detail; then I cut out a thin piece of styrene tube, attached it, and sanded it again to get the height just right. I later carefully cut out the drainage area with an Xacto knife and topped it by adding a weld around the area with stretched sprue.

I felt that the hatch attachments needed to be cut down a little, as the hatch sat way too high. Before adding the Aber part I built up the torsion bar hatch supports with styrene bits so that they would both sit evenly. This made a real difference when attaching the brass rod torsion bars.

The Jordi Rubio replacement metal barrel was another welcome upgrade, and a quick and easy replacement. The gun muzzle break was detailed by adding tiny photo-etch lifting lugs from Athabasca's brass-etch eyebolts and nuts made using my trusty Historex punch set.

The tracks

Tamiya's rubbery kit tracks are nice, but to achieve the proper sag effect so prominent on Russian vehicles of the era, I decided to exchange these for Friulmodel's beautiful individual metal tracks. I chose the early 'split-type' for this particular vehicle: there is some debate as to whether they were ever installed on this vehicle but there is photographic proof to back me up. After giving them a quick soak in soapy water, I attached the links together: Friulmodel supply the wire needed to connect the tracks together, and this needs to be measured and cut before installing.

To raise the detailing stakes, I punched out small bolts with my Historex, and set them into the tiny holes with superglue. I went further and added an extra bolt to each track link to replicate the end connectors.

Be sure to measure up the tracks beforehand, and give them a test fit. You can then install them when everything is painted. These tracks are fairly weighty and this can cause some of the more delicate parts to snap off.

After assembly, a quick coat of Tamiya primer seals the tracks for easy painting. When painting tracks, especially metal ones, it is good practice to attach a bit of wire to one end of the track length. This makes them easy to handle, and means

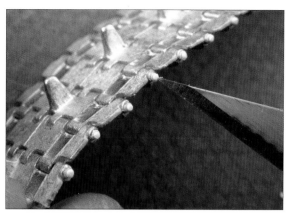

When working with Friulmodel metal tracks, I find that pre-cutting the attaching wire beforehand saves time. Connecting the tracks together is a breeze. Just insert the cut wire with a pair of pliers and trim off the excess, then add a quick drop of superglue to each link.

Friulmodel tracks are nice, especially for the sagging effect, but they are not as detailed as Modelkasten's. Adding styrene bolts to replicate the track connecting bolt will add a nice touch, but it's definitely a time-consuming process.

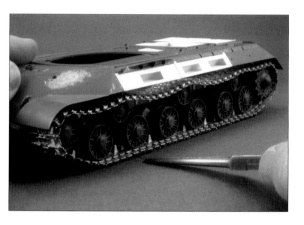

Test-fitting the Friulmodel tracks for sag and length. Note that none of the photo-etch has been applied yet.

The tracks were weathered less on this model. You can see the tracks are a nice dark brown colour.

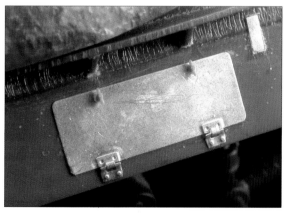

Lighter pastels were applied to both sides of the tracks, followed by a quick dry-brushing of black oils. The tracks were then set aside for installation later.

Here's a perfect example of where photo-etch falls down: wingnuts! I replaced the Aber offerings with Modelkasten's A-4 plastic wingnuts. They look far more realistic.

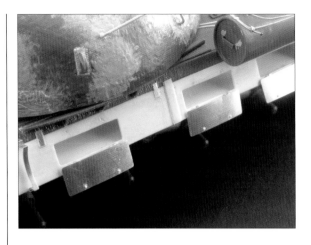

A close-up of the side bins with the Aber photo-etch. I added tiny bolts to replicate the bin closing/locking latch. I also added welds to the side superstructure bracings.

This view shows the massive saucer-like turret. The mix of Aber and scratch-built detail also shows up well in this photo.

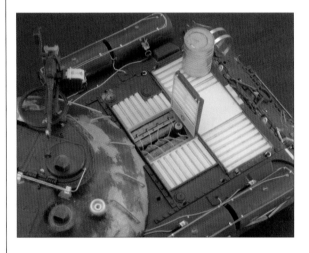

Once installed the engine sits quite nicely, with no fit problems except for some minor bracing to keep it steady. Instead of positioning the Aber smoke discharger on the cradle, I thought that just placing it on the deck would be a nice touch.

This photo shows how 'busy' the kit looks with all the detailing added. Someone asked me recently, 'How on earth do you pick that kit up?' My answer was: 'Carefully.'

they can be hung up to dry properly as opposed to having them rest on a sheet of (easily stuck to) paper. A liberal coating of Tamiya's Nato Black was applied to seal and coat the tracks, and then pastel weathering and a quick dry-brushing of oil were completed.

Painting the IS-3

There seem to have been many subtle shades of 'Russian Green' produced during the war years and beyond, so anything from a rich dark green to a light pea green colour could be acceptable. I can only surmise that whatever was at hand was used. Most IS-3s sported a rather bland paint scheme. I decided to try out a different green for this particular model, and I chose Gunze Sangyo H-73 Dark Green: its semi-gloss finish was perfect for this model.

When spraying the pre-shade coat of Tamiya Nato Black XF-69, take extra care with all the tiny photo-etch parts: they are just waiting to snap off! It is best to set the model on a piece of paper, or a turntable, and move it like so.

After the pre-shading coat, I sprayed on misty light coats of Gunze Sangyo paint.

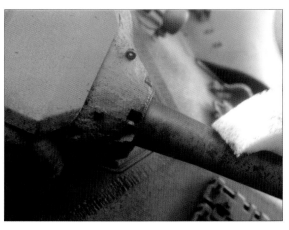

A subtle, worn, chipped effect can be achieved using the 'sponge technique' and heavily thinned Tamiya Nato Black XF-69.

The drive sprockets take to sponge-coating well, as you can see by comparing the lower left drive sprocket to the untreated one.

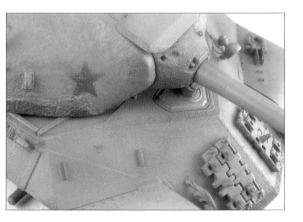

I chose the relatively simple marking of a Russian star. Instead of using the kit decals, I opted to use Eduard Express Masks XT Russian Star sheet.

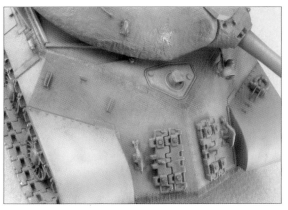

The nice effect of the sponge technique before post-shading or a final wash can be seen here.

When I was happy with the base-colour coatings, I added some subtle weathering using the sponge technique and some heavily thinned Tamiya Nato Black. This technique, if properly executed, can achieve a subtle worn and chipped effect. Once the sponged-on colour has been applied, a light misting of the original base colour will soften the harshness of the effect. Practicing is paramount to getting this technique to an acceptable standard. Playing with various paint colours and viscosity, even oils for that matter, can encourage new ideas when employing this technique.

After the final coat of base colour has been sprayed on, the turret markings can be applied.

I placed the Eduard Express mask accordingly, and misted on a couple of thin coats of Tamiya Red XF-7. I wanted a 'painted-on' feel for the markings, so I made sure that the vinyl masks weren't too flat on the surface of the turret. This gives the feathered effect I was looking for.

Next I gave the model a post-shading application, using a mixture of Tamiya Flat Black XF-1 and Tamiya Red Brown XF-64 airbrushed into corners and crevices. This softens the impact of the base colour and adds a new dimension to the overall monotone look of the model. After a few finishing touches, such as painting the smaller items, and the application of some very subtle streaking done with oils and pastels, the project was completed.

The Tamiya IS-3 has to be one of my all-time favourite tanks. It's beautifully engineered and frankly can easily be built 'out of the box' in a weekend. But if, like me, you want to update the kit to higher standards, the best solution by far is to use Aber's photo-etch set and some good replacement tracks – and a little scratch-building!

PAGES 52–55: the completed IS-3.

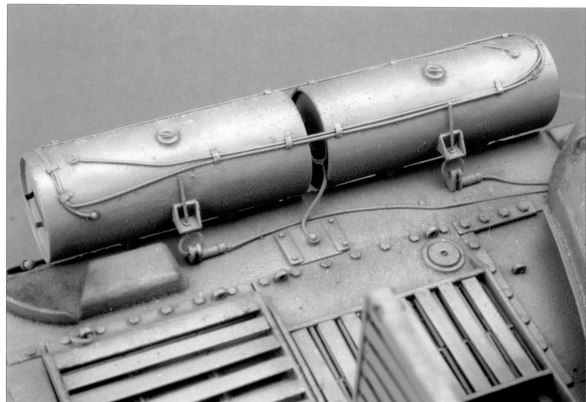

Building the ISU-152 SP Gun in 1/35

Subject:	ISU-152 (mod. 1945) Self-Propelled Gun
Model by:	Nicola Cortese
Skill level:	Advanced
Kit:	Tamiya JS-3 Stalin no. 35211
	Cromwell Models CA 79 ISU-152 resin conversion kit
Additional detailing sets used:	Friulmodel ALT-34 IS-3 tracks
	Tichy Train Groups various eyelet, nut and bolt details
	Athabasca's brass-etch eyebolts and liftrings
	Aber etch tie downs no. 35 A95
	Detail Associates brass wire
Paints:	Gunze Sangyo H-320 Acrylic Green

When considering something a little different for this book, I immediately thought of Cromwell Models' resin conversion of the rare prototype ISU-152 mod.1945 heavy assault gun. Its look was sleek, mean and radically angular, and it still looks modern today. Cromwell released their conversion kit for the Tamiya IS-III in the mid-1990s. I felt that this variant would be a good one to demonstrate restrained weathering techniques and museum-referenced build.

A little background history

Little information is available on this rare vehicle. In early 1945, with the threat of the Tiger II looming, plans were underway to develop a new Soviet assault gun to combat such large, heavily armoured vehicles. What *is* known is that this vehicle utilised the IS-3 chassis the same way the IS-122/IS-152 used the IS-2 chassis. The ISU-152 prototype featured a 152mm main gun and also had two 12.7mm DShKM machine guns, one of which was roof mounted. Unfortunately, some design features were deemed impractical and it was never approved for production. Only one ISU-152 exists today, in Moscow's famous Kubinka Tank Museum.

The Cromwell conversion kit

The kit basically consists of a two-piece, cream-coloured resin upper hull, which requires mounting on Tamiya's IS-3 lower hull. It also includes the two external fuel tanks and a few smaller resin bits. It's an impressive piece of resin, although some of the casting is a bit rough and there were a few air bubbles, especially on the smaller pieces. The most striking features are its beautiful cast texture, and its torch-cut effect where the superstructure's massive armour plates meet.

Construction
The lower hull

As described in the instructions, some minor surgery is required for Tamiya's donor IS-3 kit in the front glacis area. I carefully cut 10mm out of the front area, double-checking the area for an even fit before supergluing the two sections together.

Apart from this, the build-up was straightforward. The lower hull drive train and suspension are trouble free, except for the addition of a number of weld

I measured out 10mm, and carefully cut out the area with my Dremel. Here I'm gently scrapping off the excess plastic, making sure it will be a clean fit.

Cromwell's resin front area needs some obvious trimming: before gluing, some more dry-fitting will be required to make sure the superstructure sits straight.

beads to the front glacis and back plate sides, which were fabricated with stretched sprue and a thin application of Tamiya extra fine liquid cement.

The upper hull

The first thing I noticed when inspecting the kit was that part of the upper-hull-side pick shovel had broken off, like many pieces, particularly the small ones. Luckily I found a replacement in my spares box. With a sharp new Xacto blade, I carefully scrapped off the remainder of the moulded-on shovel, taking care not to dig too deep. I then gently sanded the area with a medium-grade sanding stick. I later applied some much needed texture to the area with several layers of Mr Surfacer 500.

Before joining the engine deck section to the superstructure halves, special care needs to be taken so that the two upper halves mate straight and evenly. Some delicate sanding is needed to ensure both halves have even, straight edges for a good fit.

The front part of the resin superstructure needed to be slightly trimmed as per the instructions. However, I decided to measure the front to make sure all was lined up perfectly beforehand. Then I proceeded to carefully trim off the excess resin with a modelling saw.

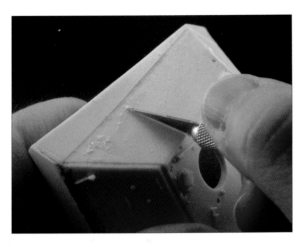

Unfortunately, Cromwell's moulded-on 'pick' tool had partly snapped off. Having removed the remainder of the unwanted piece, I carefully scraped off the excess with an Xacto knife

Mr Surfacer can also be used as filler. After a quick application, I scraped off the residue, leaving a nice smooth surface.

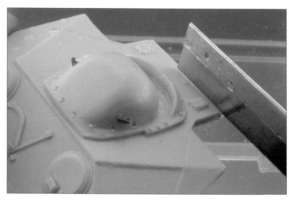

Make sure that both parts of the superstructure are straight. I've applied a couple of coats of Mr Surfacer 500 to the middle to reinforce the two halves.

Cutting the resin excess is easy with a sharp saw. When working with resin, I like to keep the resin part moist to avoid dust.

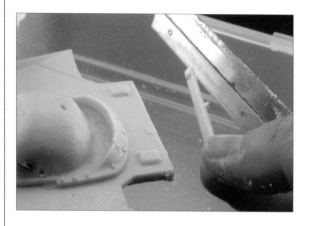

A nice even cut. The nice thing about working with resin is that the part doesn't need to be sawed all the way through: when deep enough, it can be easily snapped off. Some more sanding is required, and the piece will have to be dry-fitted to ensure the proper height.

Attaching the back part first was critical for getting the upper superstructure straight. I did have to add some height to the middle inner hull using some styrene, so that the superstructure sat evenly.

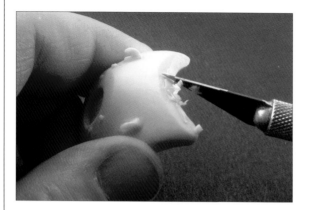

When working with resin, I find that scraping the piece with a sharp knife is a good way to reduce dust.

I wanted to add a cast texture to the gun mantlet, so I applied a couple of light coats of Mr Surfacer 500, stippled on with a nylon brush. At this point I also replaced the moulded-on tow hooks with Tamiya items from an IS-3 kit.

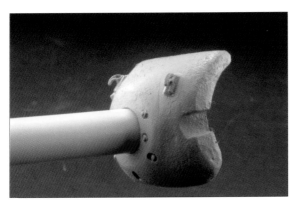

As you can see, adding texture is a subtle yet effective way to give your model an extra dimension.

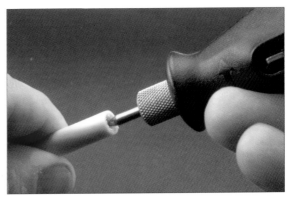

A Dremel rotary drill is a really important tool to have. Deepening the inside of the barrel a little more was easy to do.

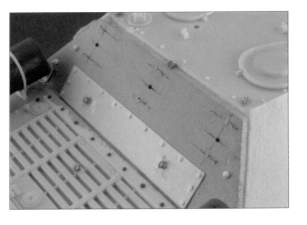

Aber photo-etch tie downs and bolts made up most of the rear detailing. I fabricated the small lower rectangular plate with 0.10 styrene sheet and bolt detail using my Historex Bolt set. The surround lifting lugs are made from 0.12 brass wire.

The Cromwell resin fuel tanks were so misshapen it was easier to replace them with extras from the Tamiya IS-3 kit. The fuel tank mounts had to be scratch-built, with photo-etch grab handles, styrene strip and bolt detail added.

I scratch-built the fuel cap by punching the appropriately sized disc made with my Historex punch set, and then added a small strip of styrene for the knob itself. The 0.20 bolts are from the Tichy Train Groups bolt set – fantastic items for all manner of scratch-built projects.

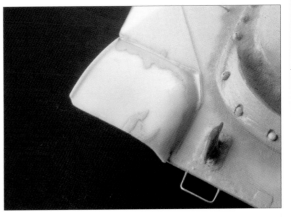

Mr Surfacer 500 was applied to the front fender outside and inside areas, layer upon layer, until all the gaps were evenly filled. This took a couple of applications. Be sure to let it dry (usually overnight) between coats to ensure a nice hard surface.

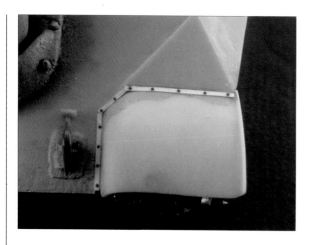

I added bolts and simulated the fender edge metal sheet with cut strips of 0.05 styrene and rivet detail from Tichy Train Groups' 0.20 rivet set.

Once installed the detailed front fenders definitely look much better and certainly add to the overall front area.

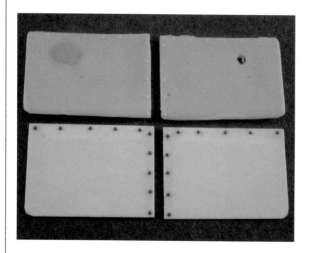

The limitations of resin moulding invariably lead to some understandable loss of detail. Styrene 0.10 plasticard and 0.20 bolt detail were used to fabricate new back fenders. As you can see, sanding the resin items could be tricky considering the small surrounding bolt detail.

As you can see from this rear view, styrene really stands out when attached to a finished model. The scratch-built fenders were carefully attached with tiny drops of superglue.

Remember to always be careful when working with resin. I generally wet any pieces for cutting or sanding in a container of lukewarm water: this helps keep dust down to a minimum.

I attached the rear part of the upper resin hull superstructure first, although some minor tweaking was needed to get it to sit right. When all was well, a couple of dabs of superglue secured it in place. Attaching the back part first was critical to getting the whole upper superstructure straight. I did have to add some height to the middle inner hull, using styrene, so that the superstructure sat evenly.

The front glacis simply slid into place, although a slight gap was evident where the initial surgery was done for the conversion. I attached the front with dabs of superglue and later filled in the tiny open area with Tamiya putty. I sealed the front area with a couple of stippled coats of Mr Surfacer 1000, giving a semi-rough-cast texture to the front hull.

The prototype 152mm ML20MS assault gun barrel and mantlet are nicely replicated although they lack cast texture. This was easily fixed with a couple of coats of Mr Surfacer 500 stippled on with a nylon brush.

When attaching the mantlet to the kit body, make sure you first drill out a hole that appears in the Cromwell kit, and then attach a 0.20 metal wire to the inside of the gun and mantlet resin part. This is to make sure it is attached evenly and has something to hold on to when set into place: superglue on its own won't do. Cromwell's resin gun barrel was a little uneven and needed some sanding and cleaning up. I also felt that the gun barrel needed to be deepened a tad, and this was easily done using my Dremel.

The Tamiya kit's mantlet tow hooks were added and I fabricated the welds with stretched sprue. Both Tamiya and Cromwell omitted the tiny tow cable spring attachments that are visible on both vehicles: luckily I found a perfect match from the spares box. I also replaced various tie downs and rivet detail on the back of the hull superstructure.

The Cromwell kit includes a resin bolted plate with lifting lugs: these were unfortunately extremely warped and deformed. I sanded down the entire area with a coarse-grade sanding stick, carefully removing all the raised resin detail, before finishing off with a finer grained stick until a smooth even surface was achieved. Some texture was then added with a coating of Mr Surfacer 500.

I replaced the fuel tanks with spares from the Tamiya IS-3 kit mainly because the Cromwell offerings were not well cast. I added all the pertinent bits with rivet and bolt detail, scratch-building the mounts with styrene strip and rod.

The front fenders are difficult to get right. After studying several photos, I concluded that Cromwell got the overall shape right, but had made a mistake on the attachment. I carefully attached the kit fenders with superglue. There were some large unsightly gaps to fill, but I didn't want to mess up the delicate surface with Tamiya putty. So I repeatedly applied Mr Surfacer 500 to the inside fender wells with a toothpick. Just dab a drop onto the area and let the capillary action do the work for you.

Here is a neat trick for when you want to sand those hard to get to or delicate areas: use nail polish remover instead! Apply it to the area using a cotton bud/Q-tip, and gently swab it until you are satisfied with the texture.

I detailed the Tamiya IS-3 tow cables by adding metal washers to the ends of each from Athabasca Scale Models' brass-etch set no. 0102, and attached them with tiny drops of superglue.

A view of the front completed with all the sub-assemblies attached. Friulmodel metal tracks have been test-fitted for proper 'sag'.

The view of the rear deck area shows the various detail additions. Larger bolt details were shaved off the Tamiya donor kit's upper hull and 0.20 brass was used in place of the kit's rear engine hatch hinge. A new pick was added to replace the kit's damaged one. I also added bolt and strip detail to the gun mantlet cover. Next I lightened up the base colour with a couple of drops of added Tamiya Flat White XF-2 until I got the contrasting effect I wanted. The road wheels and DShKM machine gun were also painted like so and left to dry overnight.

A quick pre-shade of Tamiya Nato Black XF-69 was sprayed over the entire kit. It makes a real difference, especially when working with different coloured plastic and resin.

A couple of coats of Gunze Sangyo H-320 Dark Green were applied in thin, even applications using my Iwata airbrush.

The acetone in the remover attacks the Mr Surfacer – don't worry, the resin is strong and can take repeated applications. It works with Tamiya thinner and plastic too. Remember to do this with plenty of ventilation.

As far as I can tell, the front fenders were bolted onto the hull rather than welded on as the Cromwell kit has them. The back fenders were another story completely: one of the moulded-in back fenders had already snapped off, and both were badly warped. They both also had huge sinkholes, and were frankly easier to fabricate from plasticard and bolt detail.

I added the kit tow cable as per photographs of the real vehicle in Kubinka. To ensure a uniform appearance for the hooks, a quick dab of Mr Surfacer 1000 was applied. The tow hook cable guides were made from 0.12 brass rod bent to shape as per my references and attached with superglue. I boldly removed the travel lock attachments points, reckoning that this was something never included on the real vehicle – although I may well be wrong.

Painting and weathering the ISU-152

The pick shovel was hand painted with a mix of Tamiya Red Brown and Khaki acrylics. The metal part was painted with Games Workshop's excellent Bolt Gun Metal acrylic paint.

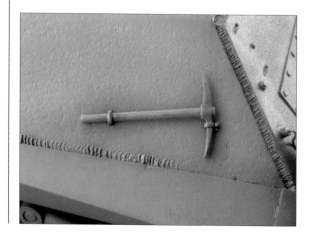

Instead of using a flat matt colour I decided to use Gunze Sangyo Acrylic Green H-320, which is semi-gloss and seemed to align best with my reference photos. These paints are a new favourite of mine, not only because they are particularly vibrant, but also because they spray on beautifully. I generally like to thin the paint about 50 per cent. Because this was a prototype vehicle, markings were probably never applied – none are visible.

I airbrushed on a healthy coat of pre-shade before moving on to the base colour. Then the smaller items like the roof-mounted DShKM machine gun, side-hull pick and tow cable were painted, prior to the wash applications. An extremely light post-shade was sprayed into corners and crevices of the model using a mixture of Tamiya Flat Black XF-1 and Tamiya Red Brown XF-64. Although I wanted to minimise the weathering, I did give the kit a number of light washes of a mix of Burnt Umber and Black Winsor & Newton oils. Pastel weathering was kept to a strict minimum, but I couldn't help adding a little 'dust' using some very light coloured pastels, just to add a bit of depth.

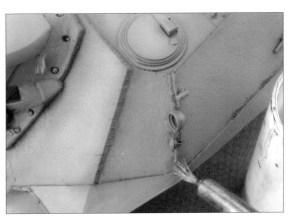

Games Workshop's Bolt Gun Metal was also used for the tow cable and tow hooks. A small piece of note-pad paper was gently placed between the two areas, making painting simple.

Post painting, a number of light washes were carefully applied to the entire model. The wash subtly increases contrast, which breaks up the blandness of the overall paint scheme.

The tracks

Friulmodel's ALT-34 IS-3 tracks were attached together as explained previously, with lengthened wire and capped with a dab of superglue. Because of the direction and the placement of the actual track attachment points, I added bolt detail to the open ends of one side of tracks. Given that this represents a museum vehicle, the tracks would be shown in pristine condition, without heavy weathering: a light pastel application was all that was required. This presents a rather interesting problem: how to recreate clean, new and realistic tracks without making them look one dimensional and bland.

Before I began painting, I attached a piece of wire to the ends of the entire length of the track, to make them easier to handle later. I post-shaded them using 80 per cent Tamiya XF-1 Flat Black/20 per cent XF-64 Red Brown mix, spraying it into the recessed areas of both sides of the track length. This also helps tone down the glossy look of the tracks, and makes them look less toy-like. A couple of applications of a dark wash of mineral spirits and diluted black oil paint helped enhance the final look. The completed tracks were installed after the main body had been painted.

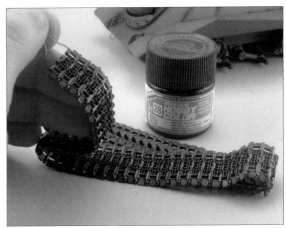

After a couple of liberal coats of Tamiya primer, I applied several coats of Tamiya Nato Black XF-69 to the track lengths making sure to get between the track links. Here is an example of what both colours look like when applied.

I found Gunze Sangyo Black Metal H-28 to be a perfect match for the actual track colour. This paint goes on smoothly and has a realistic metallic look when dry.

Cromwell's ISU-152 may not be everyone's cup of tea, but it's a perfect choice for the modeller who would like to try a resin conversion that isn't too demanding. Just think of the comments from fellow modellers when you display it – if nothing else, it's a great conversation piece!

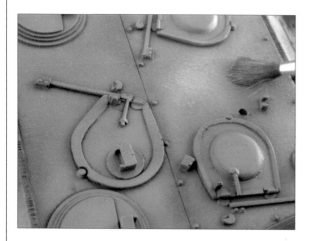

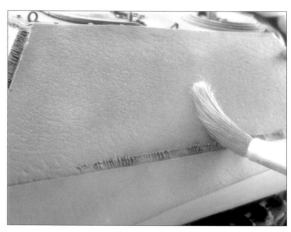

I use pastel chalks for all kinds of applications. When it comes to recreating subtle weathering, I prefer to work with lighter shades of chalk. Here a small amount is being dropped onto the top of the hull. By gently working the brush in a circular fashion, a faded and worn look can be created.

Adding pastel weathering to the side hull can look good too. I start with a small amount of pastels and work up, using different size brushes. For this application I wanted a subtle overall 'dust' effect, as opposed to a localised 'streak' effect.

PAGES 64–66: the completed ISU-152.

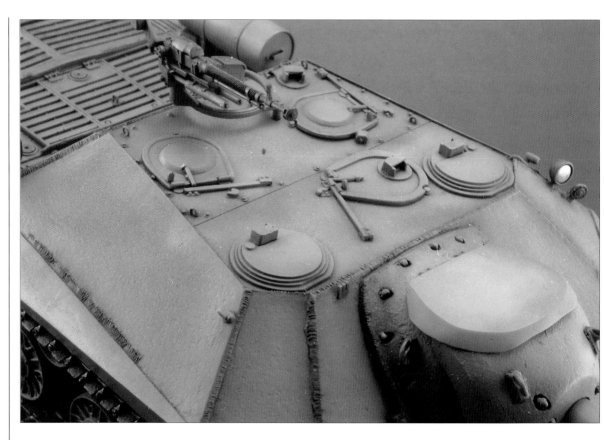

Building the IS-2 in 1/76

Subject:	IS-2
Model by:	Nicola Cortese
Skill level:	Advanced/intermediate
Kit:	Fujimi Stalin JS-2M (SWA-32)
	Fujimi Stalin JS-2 (SWA-30)
Additional detailing sets used:	Detail Associates brass wire, various sizes
	Evergreen styrene strip
	Athabasca brass-etch eyebolts, and lift rings
	K&S Metal foil sheet for the fender detail
Paints:	Gunze Sangyo H-73 Dark Green
	Gunze Sangyo H-320 Dark Green

When considering an IS-2 in small scale, I was quite disappointed with some of the 1/72-scale kits available. They weren't terrible, it's just that none really caught my eye. However, the Fujimi 1/76-scale IS-2 and IS-2M kits have delicate, crisp mouldings and I was really taken by these veritable jewels. I decided to detail one of them, and build the other 'out of the box'.

Designed by the same team at DML/Dragon, they look remarkably like a miniaturised DML/Dragon IS-2 kit. In many ways they are just as accurate. It is often noted that the IS-2M is a late-war variant of the IS-2 series, but in fact the IS-2M was developed in the mid-1950s – so this variant should really be known as just a late-model IS-2, not an IS-2M. The only real differences are the separate upper hull and mantlet types.

Detailing and enhancing the late-model IS-2 variant was an intimidating prospect to say the least: I could find no detail sets available for this scale. I decided to see what I could do with a combination of styrene, photo-etch and aluminium sheet though. I also chose to display an early IS-2, thus using the kit's nice decals.

Construction

Unfortunately, the Fujimi offerings have the same 'height' problem as the DML kits. Once again this can be fixed by slightly raising the bottom hull with a small strip of styrene. A 0.75mm spacer between upper and lower hulls is all that is needed to get the correct height – realistically, though, considering the tiny size of the kit, it is up to you to decide if the adjustment is worth it! I raised both hull sections. Other than this, these kits are easy builds with no significant problems.

The turret

On first inspection, the turret grab handles are a little on the thick side, and are moulded in as per the late-model variant. For both of the turrets, I started by filling the oddly placed glue seam where the rear turret machine gun is attached. No turret texture or welds are evident, so I quickly set to address this with a light texturing of Mr Surfacer 1000. The IS-2 family of vehicle turrets is known for its noticeable weld seam, which attaches the two-piece turret together, so I felt this was important.

I fabricated these welds with heated, stretched sprue: this is formed by taking a piece of plastic tree, or any piece of rod-like styrene, and holding each end 0.5in. above a candle or other flame for a few seconds. Be careful not to

I added fine texture with Mr Surfacer 1000. Because of the small scale I tried to avoid any heavy handedness.

This view shows the minute weld details that were carefully applied with stretched sprue.

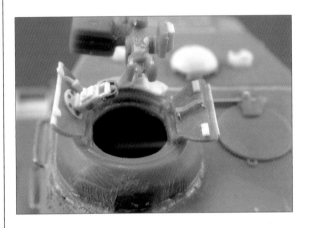

The commander's hatch was the most difficult aspect to get right. I painstakingly recreated the tiny periscope out of styrene strip and the additional tiny bolt detail was taken from the hull of an old 1/72-scale kit in the spares box. For the driver's hatch, I used cut pieces of thin wire, plus a tiny strip of Tamiya tape to replicate the leather hatch handle.

Using the 1/35-scale Dragon/DML IS-2M's machine-gun mount as reference, I fabricated a tiny version to replace the kit's rather simplistic offering.

burn it: just warm it and you'll feel it getting softer. As it softens, gently stretch it with your fingers.

Since this kit was getting the full detail treatment, I drilled out holes for the 0.10 brass rod for the turret grab handles. In hindsight, the brass replacements look a little too thick, but still look much better than the kit offerings.

I wanted both turret hatches to be displayed open: here the kit detailing is understandably simplified. My key reference for this area was *Model Detail* no.6 on the IS-2/2M Heavy Tank from Rossagraph Publishing.

I just had to find a way to have a hull-side pistol port open. Having opened up both sides with a pin vice, I closed one up, scratch-building the plug that dangles from the porthole when open. I painstakingly tried to detail up as much as I could on this kit. Some of the many hull and turret details attended to are detailed here:

- Periscopes on the turret and upper hull of the kit
- Turret ventilation dome, fabricated from stacked styrene discs

I added small, thin pieces of 0.05 styrene strip to the cradle mounts to give them a little added dimension.

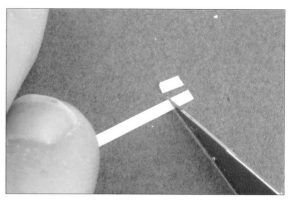

Step 1 of creating the mounts: I cut an outline of the cradle from 0.10 styrene strip. Once one had been made, I just copied the rest.

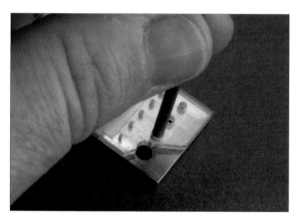

Step 2: I positioned the styrene piece under my Historex punch – which has clearly seen some action!

Although the mounts are not perfect, they'll do just fine.

- Fuel tank cradles, scratch-built from styrene
- Rear tow hook cable guides, made from 0.08 brass rod
- Turret mantlet cover, made from a combination of stretched sprue, cut to measure, and tiny 0.05 strips of styrene cut in microscopic sections for the challenging hinges
- Fuel cell cradles, using my Historex punch set

The lower hull

Injection plastic moulding can only go so far, as shown by the exhaust deck louvres, which are moulded in one piece. I decided to open up the area and add the louvres as per the real vehicle. I carefully cut open the area, measured it, and added the louvres made from Evergreen 0.10 x 0.20 plastic strip. To make things easy I added a strip of styrene to the insides of the deck portion to act as a 'step', ensuring that all the louvres sat at an equal height. It took me two attempts but it worked out well in the end.

I removed all the front fender bracings and scratch-built the tiny right fender bracing out of styrene sheet, gently twisting it to make it look battered. Leaving just one bracing on the vehicle can create a dramatic effect, especially when the massive tracks are exposed.

The kit exhaust screens are moulded on, and understandably this would be very difficult to replicate (although they look pretty good). I pushed myself for

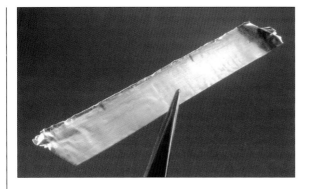

I wanted to replicate battle-damaged fenders. I basically remade a copy of the original kit fenders and then cut and measured sheet aluminium from K&S Metal foil. I mangled the front edges with pliers. Taking the cover photo of Concord Publication's *Stalin Heavy Tanks 1941–1945* as inspiration I went ahead and removed the kit fenders and carefully measured and test fitted the new aluminium replacements. Once they lined up right, they were carefully attached with small drops of superglue.

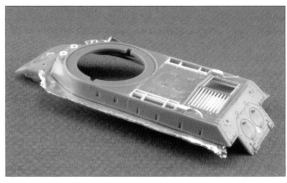

A view of the in-progress upper hull after the fenders have been installed.

The exhaust deck louvres were made from Evergreen 0.10 x 0.20 plastic strips.

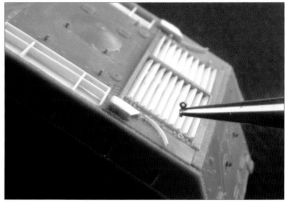

I added tiny Athabasca photo-etch eyelets to the rear deck. All they need is a tiny drop of superglue to keep them secure. Notice the subtle torch-cut effect on the rear deck plate.

weeks to figure out how to detail this area. No aftermarket set exists – and how would I be able to find acceptable exhaust screens for this scale? Luckily, my friendly hobby shop clerk procured some pretty decent workable screens from the train section, and they looked perfect. After opening up both exhaust areas, I boxed in the area with styrene sheet exactly as per the real vehicle with 0.10 styrene.

I added a small tarp just to give an added dimension to the overall look. For this, a chocolate wrapper was cut and crimped to size and drooped over the side of the hull. I find adding a tarp or some sort of 'luggage' adds to the overall realism and character of a kit.

The tracks

The kit tracks are beautiful – delicate plastic link-and-length type complete with moulded-in sag. Unfortunately, they have to be set or glued into place when painting so special care has to be taken when weathering. Straight-end nail clippers were used to detach the tracks from the sprue: if cut straight, no cleaning is required. Tweezers and a steady hand are both vital for this.

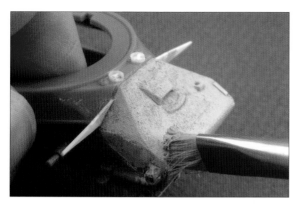

After attaching the upper and lower hulls together, a quick application of Mr Surfacer was used to seal and texture the front end.

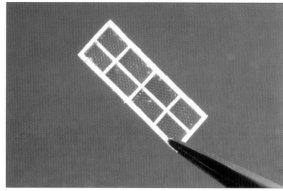

As for the bracing, I cut thin strips of 0.05 styrene sheet, which was extremely difficult because of the thinness and the frailty of the strips. I then cut and carefully attached the tiny mesh to the bracing with tiny drops of superglue.

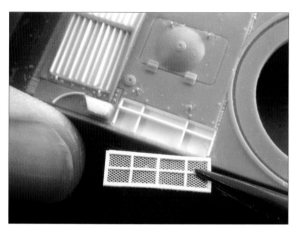

Although, a little crude and basic, and in retrospect somewhat difficult to recreate, it does improve the final look.

I attached the tracks together in two separate halves. I started with the bottom half, carefully gluing them with Testors 'slow-setting' glue.

This photo will give you an idea of the size of the wheels and tracks in relation to their 1/35-scale big brother's 'gigantic' offerings!

Before painting begins, a view of some of the various tiny hull and turret details plus the aluminium front fender.

A close-up of the back plate showing the tow hook cable guides in place. Note the tiny liftrings made from brass wire.

Although I don't have the biggest 'paws' in modelling, this photo will give an idea of the kit's tiny size.

Whether you choose to super-detail or build out of the box, either way these kits are fantastic, a testament to the great designers at Fujimi Models.

Gunze Sangyo H-320 Dark Green is sprayed onto the model using my Iwata airbrush.

The glue I used means the tracks are still malleable and they dry overnight, giving enough room to place and set them. The top half was more difficult. Be careful to:

1: Make sure the tracks are going in the right direction.
2: Follow the instructions closely.

Adding the tracks to the vehicle is pretty easy at this point. If the instructions regarding the number of links are followed, things should fall into place easily. I had no problem joining the top and bottom tracks. I simply started by putting the bottom half in place, with all the running gear in situ, then carefully sliding the top portion of the track links through the already glued return rollers.

The tracks will have to be painted after they have been attached to the vehicle, which may be a little daunting for some. When applying the post-shade don't just paint the track area. When it comes to final weathering, a light misting of Tamiya Buff will give a nice dusty effect overall.

Painting and weathering

I washed the kits in some lukewarm water with a tiny drop of washing-up liquid before getting the painting underway, and then left it to dry overnight. I don't like

(continues on page 76)

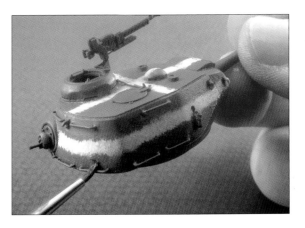

The recognition cross white lines were first roughly sprayed on with Tamiya Flat White. It was then a matter of going back and forth with a small brush, painting and covering each previous colour until I got the 'rough' effect I was happy with.

A lighter shade of the Gunze Sangyo H-320 Dark Green (with just a drop or two of Tamiya Flat White added) was sprayed on to increase contrast.

For the 'out of the box' build IS-2, Gunze Sangyo H-73 Dark Green was used. Here in the preliminary painting stages, the subtle difference in colour is evident.

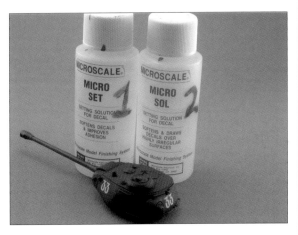

A quick brush application of both Micro Set and Micro Sol secured the tiny decals to the textured hull.

Smaller items like the front tow shackles were painted with Bolt Gun Metal.

Once the decals were on, a lighter coating of the same colour with a drop of Tamiya Flat White was applied.

After the painting and post-shade processes, a wash was applied to both kits. Here the IS-2 receives a light wash.

The kit tracks undergo the weathering process.

A brushed-on coating of Tamiya thinner is applied to the tracks, then a dark earth tone pastel was dropped on.

When the pastels are completely dry, carefully remove any excess with an old tooth brush.

Dab on a small amount of Tamiya thinner mixed with black pastels to add depth to the tracks.

Painting the tarp with Tamiya XF-49 Khaki and a steady hand: it looks a little wet but will become flat when dry.

TOP AND ABOVE: the completed IS-2M.

ABOVE AND RIGHT: the finished IS-2M in detail.

using primer on my kits, especially with etch or fine details: I just gave it my customary pre-shade of Tamiya Nato Black, sprayed on the areas where a shadow would be cast. I used Gunze Sangyo acrylics paints for both the kits. For the IS-2, I chose Gunze Sangyo H-73 Dark Green, while for the IS-2M, I opted for H-320 Dark Green: both are semi-gloss. The H-73 has a brownish hue, while the H-320 is a nice plain dark green. I added about 50 per cent Tamiya thinner to them before spraying. I used the cover photo of Concord's *Stalin Heavy Tanks 1941-1945* book for inspiration. Regarding the markings, I noticed that Russian troops would paint on simple and crude recognition crosses, sometimes without adding turret tactical numbers: I thought that this would be a good style to follow for the IS-2M.

ABOVE: the two finished models compared.

LEFT: the IS-2M's turret area in detail.

In line with my original intent, I used the kit decals for the IS-2 kit: the Gunze Sangyo paint, being a semi-gloss, accepted them without problem. I did apply both Micro Set and Micro Sol decal setting solution to the model so that the decals would properly soften and adhere to the textured hull.

Weathering was kept to a minimum on the IS-2 kit, with just a bit of mud on the front and rear lower hulls and some subtle pastels added. However, for the IS-2M, I wanted to take full advantage of the exposed track and fender detail – perfect for all sorts of heavy pastel weathering tricks! Be careful to 'scale down' the weathering, particularly if you're used to larger scale kits.

Further reading and research

There are several very good books available on the IS tanks, which I used for reference when working on this book. Some lesser known publications have come out of Russia recently, and they are quite good, but the following books are both concise, detailed and, more importantly, not difficult to get hold of.

Osprey's New Vanguard on the IS tank is written by Steve Zaloga, one of the most respected modellers and historians living today, and it comes highly recommended. It is extremely well written and provides an excellent overview of the subject.
- New Vanguard 7: *IS-2 Heavy Tank 1944–73* (ISBN 1-85532-396-6, London 1993)

The Armada series of publications are excellent, although they can be hard to get hold of in certain locations. Be warned that these books were originally in Russian before being reprinted with English text, giving rise to a few 'translation' issues – but the photos are well worth the cover price.
- *The IS Tanks*, Armada no. 6, by I Svirin.
- *Red Army Tank Camouflage 1930–1945*

The Japanese *Ground Power* magazines are fabulous little volumes packed with photos and information. Although most of the text and captions are in Japanese, they are worth acquiring for the large number of photos they contain.
- *Ground Power* issue 76: has an excellent section on the IS-2 and IS-3.
- *Ground Power* issue 77: features the ISU-152 Self-Propelled Gun.
- *Ground Power* issue 91: features the IS-3 and IS-3M.

Rossagraph Publishing has issued two fantastic volumes on the IS-2 and IS-3 respectively. Produced specifically for the armour modeller, these small booklets are packed with clear, close-up photos of details that are often overlooked.
- *Model Detail Photo Monograph 6: IS-2/IS-2M*
- *Model Detail Photo Monograph 7: IS-3*

A few other books can be recommended:
- *Stalin's Heavy Tanks 1941-1945: The KV and IS Heavy Tanks*, by Steve Zaloga and Jim Kinnear (Armor at War series, 1997).
- Military Ordnance Special no. 20: *IS-3 Stalin Heavy Tank*, by Steve Zaloga (Darlington Press).

Websites
General modelling websites
AFV Interiors   http://afvinteriors.hobbyvista.com
Hyperscale   www.hyperscale.com
Missing-Lynx   www.missing-lynx.com
Perth Military Modeling http://pmms.webace.com.au
Plastic Warfare   www.plasticwarfare.com

Russian armour websites
Achtung-Dish   www.tersys.ru/dish/index2.htm
The Russian Battlefield   www.battlefield.ru
The Russian Military Zone   http://history.vif2.ru
The Tankmaster   www.thetankmaster.com

Model manufacturer websites
Aber Photo-etch   www.aber.net.pl
CMK   www.czechmasterskits.cz
Dragon   www.dragon-models.com
Eduard   www.eduard.cz
Iwata   www.arttalk.com/iwata/index.htm
Jaguar   www.jaguarmodels.com
Tamiya   www.tamiya.com
Trumpeter   www.trumpeter-china.com

Kit availability

Scale	Manufacturer	Reference no./item name	Type	Tank name
1/35	Shanghai Dragon	Sd6803, Chinese ISU-152	Model kit	ISU
1/35	Italeri	It296, Soviet ISU-152 Self Propelled Tank	Model kit	ISU
1/35	Zvezda Models	Zv3532, ISU-152 SP Gun	Model kit	ISU
1/35	DML/Dragon Models	Dr6012, JS-2 Stalin II	Model kit	IS-2
1/35	DML/Dragon Models	Dr6018, JS-2M CHZK Stalin 2	Model kit	IS-2
1/35	DML/Dragon Models	Dr6052, Russian JS-1 (M.1943) Heavy Tank	Model kit	IS-2
1/35	DML/Dragon Models	Dr6804, JS-2M UZTM Prod. Type Stalin II	Model kit	IS-2
1/35	Italeri	It281, Joseph Stalin II	Model kit	IS-2
1/35	Shanghai Dragon	Sd6804, JS-2M UZTM Prod. Type Chinese	Model kit	IS-2
1/72	PST Models	Pst72001, JS-1 Soviet WW II Tank	Model kit	IS-2
1/72	PST Models	Pst72002, JS-2 Soviet WW II Tank 1943	Model kit	IS-2
1/72	PST Models	Pst72003, JS-2M Soviet WW II Tank 1944	Model kit	IS-2
1/76	Fujimi	Fu76065, Soviet 1942 Stalin Tank JS-2	Model kit	IS-2
1/76	Fujimi	Fu76071, Soviet 1945 Stalin Tank w/MGS	Model kit	IS-2
1/35	Accurate Armour	Att48, Joseph Stalin Type I Track	Model kit	IS-2
1/35	Tamiya	Tam35211, Stalin JS3 Heavy Tank	Model kit	IS-3
1/72	Roden	Rod0701, Russian IS-3 Stalin Tank	Model kit	IS-3
1/35	Cromwell Models	Crca079, ISU 152 1945 conversion for Tamiya IS-3	Model kit	IS-3
1/72	Roden	Rod0701, Russian IS-3 Stalin Tank	Model kit	IS-3
1/72	Roden	Rod701, IS-3 Stalin	Model kit	IS-3
1/35	CMK Czech Master	Czhb022, 122mm D-25T w/ Early Mantlet & Muzzle	Accessory	ISU
1/35	CMK Czech Master	Czhb026, 152mm ML-20 Howitzer	Accessory	ISU
1/35	Eduard Accessories	Ed35157, ISU-152 Detail Set	Accessory	ISU
1/72	Military Wheels Models	Mru301, Metal Tracks for IS-2/IS-3/ISU-152/ISU-122	Accessory	ISU
1/72	Xacto	Pqp72011, ISU-152 Detail Set	Accessory	ISU
1/72	Parts Accessories	Ptp72011, ISU-152 Detail Set	Accessory	ISU
1/35	Aber Accessories	Ab35a50, Anti-Panzerfaust Shields for T-34/35 & JS-II	Accessory	IS-2
1/35	CMK Czech Master	Czhb021, 85 mm D-5T	Accessory	IS-2
1/35	Eduard Accessories	Ed35116, JS II Heavy Tank	Accessory	IS-2
1/35	Eduard Accessories	Edxt27, IS-2 Mod. 1943 Markings	Accessory	IS-2
1/35	Eduard Accessories	Edxt28, IS-2m Tactical Mkgs Mask	Accessory	IS-2
1/35	Friulmodel	Fraw12, Set of 28 wheels for JS tanks	Accessory	IS-2
1/35	Jaguar	Ja63501, JS-2 Stalin Interior	Accessory	IS-2
1/35	Jaguar	Ja63503, Russian 122mm Ammo	Accessory	IS-2
1/35	Minimeca	Mz3518, JS/ T-34 Tow Cables (2)	Accessory	IS-2
1/35	RPM Models	Rpm00229, T-34 Engine Set	Accessory	IS-2
1/35	Show Modelling	Sm055, JS-2 Detail Set	Accessory	IS-2
1/72	Parts Accessories	Ptp 72009, IS-2 Soviet Tank Detail	Accessory	IS-2
1/35	Aber Accessories	Ab35035, JS-3 Stalin Detail	Accessory	IS-3
1/35	CMK Czech Master	Czhb025, 122mm D-25T for IS-3	Accessory	IS-3
1/35	Eduard Accessories	Ed35136, JS III Stalin	Accessory	IS-3
1/35	Eduard Accessories	Ed35571, IS-3M Detail	Accessory	IS-3
1/35	Jaguar	Ja63517, Russian JS III M Conversion	Accessory	IS-3
1/35	Jaguar	Ja63819, JS-III Fuel Tanks & Smoke Mortars	Accessory	IS-3
1/35	Royal Model	Ro151, JS III Update Set (Tamiya kit)	Accessory	IS-3
1/35	CMK Czech Master	Czhb025, 122mm D-25T for IS-3	Accessory	IS-3
1/35	Eduard Accessories	Ed35571, IS-3M Detail	Accessory	IS-3
1/35	Elefant Model Accessories	E135406g, 122mm Gun for IS-3 (TA)	Accessory	IS-3
1/35	Jordi Rubio Accessories	Jr20, Soviet 122mm D-25T	Accessory	IS-3
1/35	CMK Czech Master	Czhb023, 122mm D-25T w/ Late Manlet & Muzzle	Accessory	ISU
1/35	Accurate Armour	Att49, Joseph Stalin Type 2 Track	Replacement tracks	IS-2
1/35	Friulmodel	Fratl14, Tracks JS-II + 2 drive sprockets	Replacement tracks	IS-2
1/35	Friulmodel	Fratl34, Tracks Stalin III (JS I/II/III)	Replacement tracks	IS-2
1/35	Friulmodel	Fratl54, Joseph Stalin I, II, III Series Light Type Tracks	Replacement tracks	IS-2
1/35	Friulmodel	Fraw10, IS (Stalin) tanks	Replacement tracks	IS-2
1/35	Modelkasten	Mask09, Stalin JS-2	Replacement tracks	IS-2
1/35	Modelkasten	Mask14, JS-II Stalin Type B	Replacement tracks	IS-2
1/35	Armour Track	Tk 12, Soviet 650mm Steel Track	Replacement tracks	IS-2

Index

1. Tamiya XF-13 JA Green

2. Tamiya XF-57 Buff

3. Tamiya XF-20 Medium Grey

4. Tamiya XF-69 Nato Black

5. Gunze Sangyo H-73 Dark Green

6. Gunze Sangyo H320 Dark Green

7. Gunze Sangyo H-28 Metal Black

A note on colour

One of the most frequently asked questions concerning World War II Russian armour is 'What was the official colour of these vehicles?' The 'official' olive green colour issued to wartime vehicles was called Dark Green (4BO), which is similar to FS 34102 and to FS 24098. It seems that most Russian vehicles of the period were painted this colour, although when looking at wartime black and white photos it's difficult to tell what exactly the 'right' colour is. In reality, shades varied from a 'black green' to 'pea green'. Some IS tanks were painted with intricate three- or even four-colour camouflage schemes. The effect of weathering could also change the overall look of the vehicle, and of course during the winter months, a winter white wash was applied to these vehicles – factors that add considerable diversity.

5. Gunze Sangyo H-73 Dark Green

Most IS-3s and IS-2s sported a rather bland paint scheme. I decided to try out a slightly different green for some of my builds, such as the IS-3, and I chose Gunze Sangyo H-73 Dark Green: I felt its semi-gloss finish was perfect for these models. This paint accepts decals nicely too.

6. Gunze Sangyo H320 Dark Green

For the ISU-152, instead of using a flat matt colour I decided to use Gunze Sangyo Acrylic Green H-320, which is semi-gloss. It has a lovely vibrancy, and sprays on beautifully. I generally like to thin the paint about 50 percent.

7. Gunze Sangyo H-28 Metal Black

I used Gunze Sangyo Black Metal H-28 for the track colour of the ISU-152. This paint goes on smoothly and has a realistic metallic look when dry.

1. Tamiya XF-13 JA Green

This was chosen for the base colour for the IS-2 in 1/35. This is a nice rich colour that I've used before, and which works well in conjunction with a lighter weathering colour.

2. Tamiya XF-57 Buff

I used layers of Tamiya Buff to seal and even out darker base colours, giving an almost transparent, worn-out look to the models. Also good for creating that 'dusty' effect and adding more contrast – and perfect for the desert-scheme IS-3M.

3. Tamiya XF-20 Medium Grey

I used this for the engine bay area of the IS-2 1/35 build: it contrasted nicely with the rich green hull colour.

4. Tamiya XF-69 Nato Black

This was my usual pre-shading colour, sprayed all over the model. When scratch-building, I found a considerable contrast between light styrene and darker plastics, so the black provided an even palette for the later base colours to work on.